PORTRAITS OF BIBLE MEN VOL. 2

*Revised Edition with Discussion Questions
for Individual or Group Study*

GEORGE MATHESON
Foreword by Warren W. Wiersbe

kregel
PUBLICATIONS

Grand Rapids, MI 49501

Portraits of Bible Men by George Matheson
Volume Two—Revised and Expanded

Copyright © 1996 by Kregel Publications, a division of
Kregel, Inc., P.O. Box 2607, Grand Rapids, MI 49501.
Kregel Publications provides trusted, biblical publications for
Christian growth and service. Your comments and
suggestions are valued.

Cover and book design: Alan G. Hartman
Revision and study questions: Helen Bell

Library of Congress Cataloging-in-Publication Data
Matheson, George, 1842–1906
    Portraits of Bible men, volume two / [George Matheson].—
[Rev. and expanded ed.]
        p.   cm.
    Rev. ed. of: Representative men of the Bible. 7th ed.
1987. New York: A. C. Armstrong, n.d.
    1. Men in the Bible—Biography.   2. Bible. O.T.—
Biography. I. Matheson, George, 1842–1906. Representa-
tive men of the Bible. II. Title.
BS571.M283   1996   220.9'2—dc20   96-16868
                                                                  CIP

ISBN 0-8254-3293-6

Printed in the United States of America
1 2 3 4 5 / 00 99 98 97 96

CONTENTS

The Portraits of Bible Characters Series

PORTRAITS OF BIBLE MEN
Volume One

Adam, Abel, Enoch, Noah, Abraham, Isaac,
Jacob, Joseph, Moses, Joshua, Samuel

PORTRAITS OF BIBLE MEN
Volume Two

David, Solomon, Elijah, Elisha, Job, Ishmael,
Lot, Melchizedek, Balaam, Aaron, Caleb,
Boaz, Gideon

PORTRAITS OF BIBLE MEN
Volume Three

Jonathan, Mephibosheth, Jonah, Hezekiah,
Isaiah, Jeremiah, Ezekiel, Daniel,
John the Baptist, John, Nathanael

PORTRAITS OF BIBLE MEN
Volume Four

Peter, Nicodemus, Thomas, Philip, Matthew,
Zaccheus, James, Barnabas, Mark, Cornelius,
Timothy, Paul

PORTRAITS OF BIBLE WOMEN

Eve, Sarah, Rebekah, Rachel, Miriam,
Deborah, Ruth, Hannah, Mary (the mother of
Christ), Mary (the sister of Lazarus),
Mary Magdalene

FOREWORD

George Matheson was blind, but with the eyes of his heart he could see farther and deeper than most of us. This was especially true when it came to penetrating the minds and hearts of the great Bible characters. In my opinion, no evangelical writer, including the great Alexander Whyte, surpasses George Matheson in this whole area of Bible biography. The Bible teacher or preacher who wants to grasp the significance of these important Bible characters should read Matheson and give serious consideration to his insights.

Matheson was born in Glasgow, Scotland, March 27, 1842. Early in his life his eyesight began to fail, but he managed to complete his basic schooling with the aid of strong glasses.

From that time on, he had to have assistance with his studies, and his two sisters nobly stood by him. He earned two degrees at the University of Glasgow, felt a call to the ministry, and was licensed by the Glasgow Presbytery on June 13, 1866. He became assistant to J. R. McDuff, the well-known devotional writer, and then accepted the pastorate of the church of Innellan. He was ordained on April 8, 1868.

Like many young preachers at that time, Matheson experienced a personal "eclipse of faith" and even considered abandoning the ministry. His church officers were understanding and compassionate and advised him to stay on and give God an opportunity to deepen his faith. In due time, the young minister came out of the furnace with stronger faith and a deeper understanding of God's eternal message.

It seems incredible that a blind minister in that day could accomplish all that George Matheson accomplished. He became an outstanding scholar and theologian, as well as a gifted devotional writer and preacher. Others, of course, read to him; but it was he who assembled the materials and prepared each message. He memorized his sermon, the Scripture lessons, and the hymns; and it was said that he never missed a word! He was diligent to visit his people and enter into their joys and trials. In every way, George Matheson was a devoted pastor and preacher.

It is unfortunate that Matheson is remembered today primarily as the author of the hymn, "O Love That Wilt Not Let Me Go," because his books of devotional essays and his biographical studies are rich mines of spiritual truth for the serious Bible student. In my own sermon preparation and writing ministry, I have often turned to Matheson to discover penetrating insights into familiar verses and exciting lessons from the lives of familiar Bible characters. What George Matheson has written may not move you, but it certainly excites me!

After hearing George Matheson preach, a Scottish Presbyterian Council publicly declared: "The Council all feel that God has closed your eyes only to open other eyes, which have made you one of the guides of men." I trust that you will come to the same conclusion as you read these chapters.

WARREN W. WIERSBE

1

DAVID THE MANY-SIDED

I t is very rarely that a nation has associated all her attributes with the life of a single man. I say "rarely" to avoid the possibility of exaggeration, but I do not myself know one instance of a purely national gallery having done so. The pride of a country has generally been to have a diversified gallery—to divide her great professions among different men.

Britain places her Shakespeare in a unique position of glory, but she would not seek to claim for him a union of all the professions. She is content to behold his genius in his special sphere—the sphere of the poet. She does not insist on recognizing in him a concentration of all departments—the science of a Newton, the logic of a Bacon, the statesmanship of a Chatham, the military skill of a Marlborough. She is proud to think that in enumerating her different sources of glory she can assign each of them to a separate name.

But in that one Gallery which is not national we meet with the spectacle which is elsewhere absent. We find a people, through long centuries of its history and through devious changes of its fortune, consistently and persistently agreeing to heap upon a single individual the aggregate glories of every profession in life. Israel has fixed her affections upon an ideal whose very name expresses the object uniting all desires—David—*the beloved.*

DAVID THE OBJECT OF NATIONAL DESIRES
To claim one man as the object of all national desires is a

claim not easily sustained. It can only be supported on the supposition that this one man has passed through every national experience, has filled every sphere, has partaken of every circumstance. Accordingly, the David of Israel is not simply the greatest of her kings; he is the man great in everything. He monopolizes all her institutions. He is her shepherd boy—the representative of her toiling classes. He is her musician—the successor of Jubal and Miriam and Deborah. He is her soldier—the conqueror of all the Goliaths that would steal her peace. He is her knight-errant—bringing mercy into war. He is her king—numbering her armies and regulating her polity. He is her priest— substituting a broken and contrite spirit for the blood of bulls and rams. He is her prophet—presaging with his latest breath the everlastingness of his kingdom. He is her poet—all her psalms are called by his name.

The truth is, in the estimation of Israel, this man is a personification of the nation itself—the embodiment of her qualities, the incarnation of her spirit, the type of her destiny. A conception so unique deserves consideration. How can we better photograph the form of David than by presenting the analogy between the picture of his life and the life of ancient Israel—that Israel which saw in him a mirror of her own soul.

DAVID THE MIRROR OF ISRAEL'S SOUL

Even the history of Israel seems to repeat itself in David. What do we see at the outset of his life? A shepherd boy with a very unlikely prospect of success and a very big presentiment of glory! Like the nation, he was born to a pastoral life; he fed his father's sheep on the plains of Bethlehem. Like the nation, he was deemed, in his morning, very insignificant. He had seven brothers who were strong, stalwart, gigantic men. These were pointed to as the men who would serve their country. Little David was, like little Israel, a pygmy among the giants; and the world said, "He will never equal his brothers." Yet little David had an ambition within his soul that made his brothers' ambitions look only like a molehill.

David, like his tiny country, had a dream of empire—that dream which had its beginning when Abraham heard his mission under the Chaldean stars. He, like Abraham, had received a prophetic voice, had felt the touch of an anointing hand. Ever, amid the bleating of the sheep, there had sounded in his ear a deep refrain, "You will be king of Israel! You will be king of Israel!" He kept the dream in his heart; he told it not; but all the warmer did it burn because it could not be spoken.

DAVID'S MUSIC AND KING SAUL

And though it could not be spoken, it could be sung; it made songs without words. It tuned the strings of David's harp; it accompanied his music; it imparted to his notes a wild dash and daring which made them seem to strike the stars. He was unconscious of their power; he played spontaneously—played to relieve himself. But just on that account he was overheard; unconscious genius ever is overheard. Men stood and listened in the night to the great musician. They spread his fame. They told how a nightingale had come. They spoke of a harp with chords inspired.

And by and by the tidings reached the most august ear in all the land. They came to the royal palace; they were heard by Saul the king. Saul was passing through an hour of mental darkness. There had come to him, as there comes to many of us, an unaccountable unrest. We are told of a peace that "passeth understanding"; there is also a dispeace that "passeth understanding." There are clouds in the mind which are not explained by clouds in the sky, for they often come in our days of outward sunshine.

Saul had such an experience. He was afflicted from within—afflicted in the midst of his exaltation, on the pinnacle of that proud height to which fortune had raised him. Material conditions had not caused the malady; material conditions could not remove the malady. Might not immaterial conditions be tried? If the disorder originated from within, might it not be conquered from within? Might not music have power to minister to a mind diseased? Why not call in the aid of this wonderful player whose powers of melody were reported everywhere? Why not send for David!

DAVID'S CALL COMPARED TO ISAAC'S

David is sent for and comes; and, as he comes, the Gallery repeats in him another of its past stages. He has already heard the call of Abraham; he is about to experience the call of Isaac.

The call of Abraham was the summoning to a life of glory; the call of Isaac was the summoning to a life of domestic ministration. When David entered the house of Saul, he abandoned, for the time, his dream. He laid aside his desire to rule; he tried to serve, to dig wells of comfort for the heart of another. And not without success. As he played, the malady of Saul subsided; the clouds parted, and a stream of sunshine burst upon his soul.

If a pupil in a Sunday school were asked, "Who was the first man influenced by the psalms of David?" he would not go very far wrong if he answered, "Saul." It is true that these melodies were songs without words, but they were not songs without thoughts. On the poor wandering soul of the monarch they had all the effect of a sweet and solemn prayer; they said, "Peace! Be still!" They were the earliest psalms of David—psalms of unspoken words, psalms of undefined comfort, psalms whose divine message came only in music. When the critics have disposed of all the rest, they will leave to the minstrel these first chords.

DAVID'S CALL COMPARED TO JOSEPH'S

And now the scene changes once more, and there is repeated another past phase of the Hebrew Gallery. The experience of David has echoed the call of Abraham and the domestic ministration of Isaac; it is now to echo the troubles of Joseph. He has had the dream of empire; he has had the stage of domestic life; he is now to have the experience of private jealousies—jealousies of which, like Joseph, he is to be not the sharer but the victim. There is a passion which music cannot quell, which culture cannot calm, which art cannot allay; it is envy.

In the court of Israel the personality of the young minstrel is magnetic; he draws all eyes; he wins all hearts. Men begin to contrast his face of morning brightness with the dark and lowering countenance of their monarch. Saul awakes from his nervous derangement and looks round. He sees the situation at a glance. He is losing ground; he is being superseded in the affections of his people—superseded by a stripling! He must remove this center of magnetism from the eyes of men.

What is Saul to do? How is he to get rid of David? By open violence? No; that would be unpopular. He will follow the method of Joseph's brethren; he will cause him to disappear by seeming accident. He will make him captain of a thousand men; he will send him into the front of battle, into positions where death will be almost inevitable. By means that will waken no suspicion he will remove this shepherd boy.

But the means are all in vain. David at the head of the thousand is only more magnetic still. He performs deeds of prowess and becomes the right hand of Israel. What is to be done with this troublesome prodigy? A new device presents itself to the mind of Saul, or so at least I read the narrative. (I think the incident recorded in 1 Samuel 18:11 a misplaced anticipation of that recorded in 1 Samuel 19:10.) He will simulate a return of his malady. He will pretend to be again mad, and in this seeming madness he will give David his deathblow.

Again the project fails; the musician eludes the javelin. Did the penetrating eye of David see through the subterfuge? I think it did. Be this as it may, the mask is now withdrawn. The baffled monarch turns at bay and begins his direct pursuit. He has failed in strategy; he will take direct means to rid himself of this rival. David is warned—warned from within the palace, warned by Saul's own son.

There is but one refuge—flight. David disappears from court. He wanders a while in the secluded parts of Israel. But no part of Israel is secluded enough to screen him from the eye of Saul. He must fly farther. He must leave his country altogether. He must become a stranger in a strange land. Again the national history repeats itself in David. He, like his country, becomes an exile and wanders in the land of Egypt. He treads a foreign soil; he is a fugitive and an outcast; he is indebted to the charity of others. He is oppressed and weary, now on the mountain, now in the vale—today skirting a ravine, tomorrow lurking in a cave—sometimes alone in the wilderness, sometimes within touch of his adversary. At one moment he is seen in Philistia; at another he treads the mountains of Engedi; at a third he is by the waters of the Dead Sea. The sea of his own life is dead; he has hung his harp on the willows; he has resolved to sing no more.

DAVID'S LIFE COMPARED TO JOSHUA'S
Then the curtain rises anew, and the life of David continues to repeat the history of Israel. After the Exile comes the Exodus;

after the land of bondage comes the conquest of Canaan. David's life has hitherto been itself a harp of many strings. Each chord has renewed the existence of some bygone age of the national annals. He has begun with the shepherd life of Abel. He has received the anointing mission of Abraham. He has served at the domestic hearth with Isaac. He has experienced the envy that assailed the life of Joseph. He has passed into that exile where dawned the day of Moses. He is now to emerge into that struggle which secured the land to Joshua and to repeat in his own life the transition from exile into empire.

Nor is there wanting a point of resemblance between the conquest by Joshua and the conquest by David. In both cases there is an absence of personal glory. I have shown this in the case of Joshua; it is even more marked in the case of David. It is not really David's prowess that wins him the kingdom; it is the trend of circumstances—or, as men would then have called it, the hand of the Lord.

The battle which shattered the fortunes of Saul was not fought by David—was not fought even in the interest of David. It was the Philistines that made room for David in Israel—made room without meaning to do so. It was on the field of Gilboa that the pride of Saul was extinguished—a field on which Israel and Philistia fought for their own ends. That battle almost annihilated the house of Saul. He perished; three of his sons perished; the flower of his army perished. Israel was in the position of England after the Wars of the Roses. She had lost "the last of the barons, the last of the great leaders on whom Saul's house could depend." Any strong hand would be sure to hold the reins in a nation so struck with panic. Yet, even in this panic-struck nation, the strong hand of David did not at once become supreme.

There was a lingering loyalty to the house of Saul. Eleven of the tribes clung to his memory and enthroned his son. One tribe alone declared for David—the tribe of Judah. For seven years there were two kings in Israel, each claiming undivided empire. For seven years there was internecine war between David and the remnant of Saul's house; and, though the balance of success inclined to David, his final triumph came not from his sword. It came from an act of desertion on the part of an enemy, from the abandonment of the house of Saul by one of its leading supporters.

On the whole, I am disposed to think that David realized his mission mainly by the grace of God; or, if you prefer its rationalistic equivalent, mainly by the stream of tendencies which converged in place and time so as to effect the issue. His stage of climax was the stage of Joshua. The walls of his Jericho happened to fall precisely at the moment when he happened to blow the trumpet. He was little more than a spectator of the scene which crowned him. His merit was in waiting for the tide and taking the tide. He was never more humble than on his road to the throne.

DAVID'S CHARACTER REVEALS THE CHARACTER OF THE NATION

I have thus sought to institute a parallel between the history of David and the history of the Jewish race. The evolutionist tells us that in the stages of birth the human individual passes through the phases of the ascending animal series from the fish to the mammal. I think the individuality of David repeated the history of its human ancestors—incarnated within itself the previous life of the nation. But it is not only David's history that reveals the collective life of Israel; his character does so too.

There is not in all biography a more remarkable delineation than the character of David. We have pictures of strikingly good men; we have pictures of singularly bad men; we have pictures of men who are half-good and half-bad. None of these designations will cover David. Measured by a Christian standard, he is no saint. Measured by a heathen standard, he is no sinner. Measured by any standard, he is no mixture—he never exhibits a blending of good and bad. How, then, shall we describe him? If he is not a telescope of uniform sublimities nor a microscope of uniform littlenesses nor yet a union of telescope and microscope in which one eye can see the sublime and the other the small, what is he?

He is a kaleidoscope. He reveals a series of seemingly disconnected scenes of which the later often reverses the picture given by the earlier. In each scene appears not a phase of the man, not a quality of the man but the whole man. Yet the David of today is often a direct contrast to the David of yesterday; but for his face and form we should not recognize him.

Yesterday, he had one pure spiritual friendship—the devotion to Jonathan; today, he has many sensuous loves. Yesterday, he was modest and retiring; today, through vanity, he vaunts the number of his fighting men. Yesterday, he was open and confiding; today, he deceives his benefactor Achish. Yesterday, he was chivalrous to his enemies; today, if the passage is genuine, he denies forgiveness to his greatest general. Yesterday, he saved the life of Saul, his foe; today, he takes the life of Uriah, his friend.

THE QUESTION OF DAVID'S CHARACTER

How came such a character to exist? Is there any connection in its acts beyond what is effected by the shaking of life's kaleidoscope? Can we account for a phenomenon seemingly so grotesque and really so contradictory?

I think we can. I believe this man epitomized not only the past history but the past passions of Israel. I believe the two streams of heredity which had run in separate channels through the path of the nation met at last in a single life—the life of David. If I were to christen these two streams, I should call them "The Lion" and "The Lamb."

Look back over the history of the Hebrew race; you will find the moral life of that race ever depicted as a strife between two. Go where you will, you are ever confronted by a pair. Every lamb has its opposing lion. Abel has his Cain; Abraham has his Lot; Isaac has his Ishmael; Jacob has his Esau; Joseph has his "Brethren"; Moses has his Amalek; Joshua has his Achan.

In David the two pass into one. He becomes the heir to a double heredity. The strings of his life-harp are swept by two impulses—a south wind and a north—the one bringing music, the other, discord. When you see him proceeding from the altar of God to a life of sensuality, it is not correct to say that he has had a fall from grace? If you walk through a town being newly developed and at certain parts come to vacant spaces, will this prove that the city is losing its inhabitants? It will prove the reverse. These vacant spaces are the survivals of yesterday. They suggest that yesterday there were no buildings at all—that the present amount of population has been planted on spots which were originally in the same condition.

So is it with the bad deeds of David. They are survivals of an old time—not falls from new grace. Not all at once could the city of God be built within him. Not all at once could the barren swamps be filled with homes and hearths of culture. Not all at once could the wild beasts of the forest be rooted out and the voice of Man be made to echo through the waste places. Not all at once could the forms of the past that lived within him die— the violent Cain, the wild Ishmael, the selfish Lot, the reckless Esau, the deceitful brethren of Joseph. These remained as the memories of yesterday; they waited the expansion of the city to clear them away.

THE HEART OF DAVID

Here, then, was a region in which David was not king—the region of the heart. I mean, his own heart. He had a power of captivating the heart of others, but he never took captive his own. All the winds of the past strove for the mastery of that great sea. Each prevailed in turn. Sometimes it was swept by the gust of anger, sometimes by the blast of impurity, sometimes by the storm of doubt, sometimes by the breeze of generous sympathy. At morning it caught the glow, at noon the glare, at evening the gloom. It was the heart of a child; the impression of the moment ruled it.

David felt the weakness and cried out for a king over himself. He called aloud for some one mighty enough to still the tempest of his heart. This is the deepest note of his whole biography— his distrust of himself, of his own power, of his own judgment. I do not wonder the hymns of Israel are called the psalms of David; they reflect him, they mirror him—mirror most of all his distrust of himself. When they cry, "I have made the Most High my Refuge!"—when they exclaim, "O God my Shield, look on the face of Thine anointed!"—when they pray, "Hide me in the secret of Thy pavilion!" do we not hear the refrain of that life which could find no help but in God?

There is not in the whole Gallery the picture of a soul so conscious of its weakness. David will do nothing without God. He will neither lead an army nor build a temple without the preliminary Voice. He has no confidence in his own will. Saul had confidence in his own will. He was a weaker man all round, but he rarely felt the need of the Lord. David has in his veins the strength of two conflicting streams of heredity, yet his deepest sense is that of his own nothingness. His name has become almost a synonym for the conviction of personal sin.

DAVID'S SENSE OF MORAL IMPOTENCE

And do you not see that David's sense of moral impotence has originated precisely in the strength of the contending elements within him? Had there been only one element—whether good or bad—he would never have felt that impotence. Had he been simply an amiable, passionless creature untempted by violent impulses and unassailed by the glitter of vice, he might have done less harm to his generation; but he would never have cultivated his special flower—the thirst for God.

Why is this man ever longing in a dry parched land where no water is? Precisely because his was not an untempted nature. He wanted to be good, but he could not. He had too big an inheritance of past corruption to believe in his own strength. His thirst for God came from his personal experience of the meagerness of his own soul. A placid nature would never have felt the impotence and would never have known the thirst; he would have failed to cultivate David's special flower.

David stands in the Gallery with a unique message—that the forces of the natural world are not sufficient to make a man good. It is the message commonly called evangelical. The man who preaches it from his heart must ever be one who has come fresh from the storm. He who knows not the power of passion, who feels not the seductions of sense, who never sails except on summer seas may say indeed, "Give us our daily bread," but will find little need to say, "Deliver us from evil."

If David is to cultivate the flower whose "language" is that prayer, he will have to hear the roar of the breakers and experience the crash of the timbers and learn what it is to utter the piercing cry, "Save us; we perish!" That was the education adapted to him; that was the education he received. To the city of his habitation he was led by a rough way, because the rough way was for him the only right way; his mission was to proclaim the heart's need of God.

A PRAYER

My heart needs You, O Lord, my heart needs You! No part of my being needs You like my heart. All else within me can be filled by Your gifts. My hunger can be satisfied by daily bread. My thirst can be allayed by earthly waters. My cold can be removed by household fires. My weariness can be relieved by outward rest. But no outward thing can make my heart pure.

The calmest day will not calm my passions. The fairest scene will not beautify my soul. The richest music will not make harmony within. The breezes can cleanse the air, but no breeze ever cleansed a spirit. This world has not provided for my heart. It has provided for my eye; it has provided for my ear; it has provided for my touch; it has provided for my taste; it has provided for my sense of beauty—but it has not provided for my heart.

Provide for my heart, O Lord! It is the only unwinged bird in all creation; give it wings, O Lord! Earth has failed to give it wings; its very power of loving has often dragged it in the mire. Be the strength of my heart, O Lord! Be its fortress in temptation, its shield in remorse, its covert in the storm, its star in the night, its voice in the solitude! Guide it in its gloom; help it in its heat; direct it in its doubt; calm it in its conflict; fan it in its faintness; prompt it in its perplexity; lead it through its labyrinths; raise it from its ruins! I cannot rule this heart of mine; keep it under the shadow of Your own wings!

For Further Study and Reflection

1. How is David's life as a shepherd like the early life of the nation of Israel?

2. How does David's life parallel that of Isaac? of Joseph? of Joshua?

3. How is David's character seen in the symbols of the lion and the lamb?

4. Why did David's heart cry for a king over himself?

5. How do David's past passions and corruption feed his thirst for God?

2

SOLOMON THE WISE

I n standing before the picture of Solomon, I am conscious of an impression which I have not hitherto experienced—an absence of the dramatic element. All the previous figures have stood in critical situations. Adam in the Garden, Abel in the field, Noah in the presence of the divine judgment, Abraham in his arduous mission, Isaac in his life of domestic sacrifice, Joseph in his dungeon, Moses in his desert, Joshua in his wars, Samuel in his call to imperil his worldly prospects, David in his exile from home and country—all have exhibited the spectacle of difficulty and danger. In Solomon we have a life where the difficulty and danger are not exhibited. They are there; but they are unseen.

What we do see in the foreground is an event which will be found to pertain to the life of every young man in the world—the choice of a profession. Solomon is asked, as many boys and all youths are asked, what he would like to be. He was already a king, but one may be a king in many ways. Solomon is asked what gift he would chiefly prize as a sign of real greatness. There is spread before his fancy what is spread before the fancy of all romantic young men—a choice of golden possibilities. Would he be rich? Would he be powerful? Would he be famous? Would he be an object of admiration? Would he be a wise man, a man of prudence and sagacity? Solomon says, "Let me be wise."

This seems a very commonplace introduction to a great life. But is it? It is undramatic, no doubt; it is homespun. But what if the crisis of national history has shifted from the theater to the home? What if in the transition from David to Solomon the drama of human life has itself assumed an undramatic garb? What if the possibility of tragic issues has begun to lie not in war of nations, not in rise of dynasties, not in political combinations but just at the fireside and around the family hearth? Would not this alter our view of the commonplaceness? Would it not lead us to reconsider our estimate of the Gallery's introduction to the life of Solomon— to ask if, after all, there may not be something in this narrative as rich in possible tragedy as was the threatening of a deluge or the resistance to an Egyptian bondage? Now, I am prepared to show that it was so—that Solomon's choice of a profession was really one of the most tragic acts of Jewish annals, an act on whose decision was suspended an issue as momentous as ever hung on the prayers of Moses or on the sword of Joshua.

SOLOMON'S CHOICE

Did you ever ask yourself what is the reason that the decision made by Solomon is so highly commended? To me the answer seems clear. His decision is applauded not mainly because it was a proof of personal character but because it furnished the hope of escape from a national danger. If Solomon had set his heart either upon riches or upon military glory, there would have been no guarantee that the silent mine beneath his feet would not explode. For, there was a mine beneath his feet. Peaceful as looked the scene, calm as were the surroundings, there were subterranean fires which one thoughtless deed might bring to the surface.

There was, below the crust of the soil, an underground heat which any moment might be fanned into flame by a giddy head or an unsteady hand. The only security from the warmth below was to have absolute coolness above. A hot-headed sovereign, a man on the throne animated by personal motives, would be certain at some point to fire the train. There was wanted on the seat of royalty a balanced mind, an impersonal mind, a mind in whom all private ambitions were subordinated to zeal for the common good. Let us consider this necessity a little more in detail.

THE DIVIDED KINGDOM

I said that when David came into the undivided possession of the empire, Israel was very much in the position of England after the Wars of the Roses. There had been a slaughter among the great leaders. The land was like a steed that had lost his rider; it was moving aimlessly; it was directed nowhere.

David obtained the supremacy without a rival, and he transmitted the kingdom to his son. But you will commit a great mistake if you imagine that the party of Saul was crushed because his house was crushed. I hold very strongly that the eleven tribes who followed Saul never submitted to David in their hearts.

Poor Rehoboam gets the credit of having split the kingdom into two; I do not believe it was ever really one. It was never anything more than a patched garment. Judah and Benjamin were never truly united. Their union was like the assembling together of an audience to hear a great preacher. David was the preacher. The audience had no bond of brotherhood—not even the acceptance of the preacher's doctrine. They were kept together simply by the spell of a presence, by the power of a personality, by the commanding chords of a human voice. It was a frail and impotent thread on which to suspend a kingdom

For now the voice of the preacher is still. His presence has been withdrawn; another stands in the place he used to occupy. David is dead, and a man of different mold has mounted the rostrum. Will Solomon sway the masses as David did? By natural gifts, no. The new preacher has not the elements of the old.

In every respect David and Solomon are contrasts. David was extemporaneous; Solomon is elaborately prepared. David spoke in outbursts; Solomon deals in rounded periods. David was unconventional; Solomon is steeped in culture. David appealed to human experience; Solomon expounds abstract principles. David revealed the man; Solomon exhibits the scholar. David was the sermon; Solomon lives the sermon. Clearly, if each is to be judged by his natural powers, the second cannot keep together the audience of the first.

SOLOMON'S PROBLEM

To drop the metaphor, young Solomon had a problem before him. He had to ask himself the question, How shall I keep this already disunited mass from showing its disunion? It was clear to him that to effect this he needed a very special gift—a gift quite distinct from the power of making money or the brilliancy that wins fame. I think, indeed, that the task before Solomon was the greatest that can be imposed on any king and that the man who performs it deserves to be reckoned among the greatest of all sovereigns. We are generally in a mistake on this matter.

We are under the impression that to be a king in times of open revolution is a more arduous thing than to be a king in times of unexpressed dissatisfaction. It is the reverse. In times of open revolution a sovereign requires but one power—an adequate army. But when the currents are underground, when the factions are invisible, inaudible, undefinable, when the ferment of discontent is working below the surface and the subterranean heat is making no sign, he who guides the state must have the powers of a prophet. He must have the gift of imagination, the gift of insight, the gift of anticipative sympathy, above all, that gift which defies definition— the thing called tact. The man who can preserve tranquillity among elements of inward discord is every inch a king.

SOLOMON'S PEACEFUL REIGN

Now, remember that for nearly forty years this was what Solomon did. His is characteristically the reign of peace; there is not such a period of protracted peace in all the Jewish annals. This in itself would not be a matter of greatness; there is a calm which comes from lethargy—from the absence of vital force. But the peace of Solomon's reign is the peace of a river; it is calm not through stagnation but through balanced movement. It is a peace produced in the midst of natural anarchy, in a sphere where elements tend to stand apart from one another. It is a result achieved not by the suspension of regal force but by the prolonged operation of that force.

The spectacle afforded to the eye is one of power—of greater power than could be evinced by any military conquest. The military conquest requires an effort suited to the emergency; the preservation of tranquillity amid turmoil needs an energy uniform at all times.

SOLOMON AND QUEEN ELIZABETH I COMPARED

Were I to put the question, Was Queen Elizabeth or Charles I the greater sovereign? there is not a schoolboy who would not answer, "Queen Elizabeth." But why do we hold that the earlier is more worthy of praise than the later ruler? Is it because Elizabeth was fortunate and Charles was not? No; our judgment would be quite the same if Charles had won the field of Naseby and leveled his enemies with the dust. The merit of Elizabeth lies in the fact that under her the Revolution never look place. She had elements of discord in her kingdom as fierce as any which marked the reign of Charles, but Charles let them explode; Elizabeth kept them quiet. We pronounce Elizabeth the greater potentate because her power went deeper down than the power of Charles would have gone even had it been victorious; it could retain an empire in tranquillity when everything conspired to make a conflagration.

Now, I have always felt that there is a strong historical parallel between the portrait of King Solomon and the portrait of Queen Elizabeth. I do not know of any two characters living at so wide a distance from each other in space and time who present such a remarkable analogy in their public lives. Both had a very remote prospect of reaching the thrones which they eventually secured. Both attained their position through storm and stress. Both came to a kingdom in which the democracy had been elevated to power through the fall of great families. Both ruled over a state thick-sown with secret dissensions—a state where hostile parties nursed their unspoken jealousies. Both for almost an equal period kept down public disquiet without any display of authority and without any exercise of severity.

I am tempted to add one parallel more. Both almost at the last heard the beginnings of a long-suppressed storm—a storm which their successors were to hear with appalling clearness; and the one reign, like the other, had an evening bereft of gold. The marvel in each case is not that the evening should have been dim but that the hours of the day should have continued so long bright. Nothing could be a stronger testimony to the greatness of either sovereign.

SOLOMON'S CHARACTER

Turning now exclusively to Solomon, let us observe the means adopted by him which, in securing this internal tranquillity, succeeded so long and so well. And, first of all, I wish to direct attention to the fact that his whole life is built upon a plan.

We are under a widespread misapprehension as to the character of Solomon. The popular view is that he is the delineation of a double personality—a life divided between wisdom and folly. We picture a man alternating between the cares of state and the pleasures of the sensualist. We figure him as swayed by two opposite impulses—the proclivities of the statesman and the tendencies of the man of idleness; and we are disposed to regard the latter as the reaction from the former. Now, this is not the view I take of the life of Solomon.

To me Solomon presents the picture of one man. Every incident of his life is the expression of one and the same tendency. I do not think he ever deviates from his political purpose nor ever forgets it for a moment. That he went far astray in his pleasures, that he was not always loyal to his religion, that he was unduly prodigal in his expenditure, I freely admit. But his errors were political errors. They were not moments of reaction from state cares; they were themselves part of his state policy. That they were mistakes, no one will deny; but they were mistakes of the king rather than of the man. They were committed in the pursuance of his plan of statecraft, not in the forgetfulness of it. That plan of statecraft never varied in its aim—to keep dormant that faction of the kingdom which still, with firmly held loyalty, clung to the memory of the house of Saul.

SOLOMON'S METHODS

How was this to be done? One or other of two methods was available—the awakening of a common danger or the suggestion of a common interest. The former has been the usual method of kings in the circumstances of Solomon; they have sought to purchase domestic peace by the incurring of foreign war. A nation divided by factions has often been driven into unity by the call to arm against another nation. It was so with the France of 1792; it was so with the Germany of 1870.

Many a despot has found outside war conducive to his indoor peace and has not scrupled to strike the match of international discord. A foreign irritant has often produced a home sedative, and the producing of a sedative by this means has often been a policy. It was the successful policy of Napoleon the Great; it was the attempted policy of Napoleon the Little. But it was not the policy of King Solomon.

Solomon felt that to cure strife on the homeopathic principle was but a poor salvation—that to heal domestic discord by outdoor discord was but a superficial gain. He wanted peace all round—peace not only in the inner parts but on the borders and at the gates. Accordingly, he chose another way—what seemed to him a more excellent way.

Rejecting the aid of a common danger, he turned for support to a common interest. It seemed to him that he could best bind the heart of Judah to the heart of Benjamin, that he could best reconcile his own tribe with the refractory eleven tribes, by presenting to them a positive rather than a negative ground for union. It was for this that he strove through all the years. His whole reign was an application of his principle. Sometimes he chose right measures, sometimes wrong; but with the principle itself he was never inconsistent. There is no side of his character which does not bear the stamp of this peacemaking design.

SOLOMON'S MARRIAGES

Take the domestic side. Here he is decidedly reprehensible. The vast number of matrimonial alliances which he personally and simultaneously contracted are a disgrace to family life; and even for an Eastern monarch, they place him in a low moral category. Yet I do not believe that their dominant motive was sensuality. I think his design was that the family of David should branch out in as many directions as possible at home and abroad. He felt that a common interest is greatly promoted by a common blood. He felt that nothing would weaken the memory of the house of Saul like consanguinity to the house of David.

The more branches the Davidic tree could shoot forth in the land of Canaan and the adjacent lands, the more would it be endeared to Semitic eyes. This, I believe, was the motive, the main motive, which lighted the myriad nuptial torches of Solomon. His marriages, regular and irregular, had a political aim. They were meant to graft his blood upon the Hebrew race, to connect that race for the future with his name and lineage, and to elicit the verdict of the generation yet unborn, "The whole land of Israel has a stone in the house of David."

SOLOMON'S COMMERCIAL ENTERPRISES

Take the commercial side. Here at first sight Solomon appears to be the typical moneymaker, living exclusively for the wealth he can gather. He seems to have deserted the choice of wisdom for the choice of gold. His ships travel the seas in search of merchandise; they touch at every port where the spirit of commerce dwells. His caravans range the land in the service of the trader; they go forth with native produce and return with foreign treasure. His commercial enterprise extends to all regions. It visits Tyre. It reaches Arabia. It trades with Egypt. It has business with Babylon. It probably touches the shores of India.

To outward appearance, the whole aim of his life and of his labors is the amassing of wealth, the acquisition of personal gain. But look deeper, and you will form another view. You will come to the conclusion that, to his mind, the value lay in the pursuing, not in the thing pursued. You will come to see that this itself had for him a political value. The aim of Solomon was to keep the mind of the nation in united employment. Civil war would keep men in disunited employment. But the battle of human industries was a battle which his people might all fight side-by-side.

Commercial enterprise loomed before the eye of Solomon not so much in the light of a personal gain as in the light of a popular attraction. Here was an object on which the admirers of the house of Saul and the adherents of the house of David might unite! Here was a cause in which they might work together! Here was at once a labor and a pleasure in whose pursuit each might forget its wrongs and become the ally of the other. And when the result of this commercial prosperity should appear, when the opulence of the nation should be manifested in its magnificent pageants and its splendid buildings, here was a source of common pride to Judah and Benjamin, a work whose triumph both could claim and whose glory each could share.

SOLOMON'S WISDOM IN BUILDING THE TEMPLE

But it is on the religious side that the wisdom of Solomon is most resplendent. I do not, of course, speak of those concessions to idolatry which tarnish his later years. I believe these to have been mistaken attempts at conciliation—things in which the wisdom of Solomon failed. But that which exhibits the true religious sagacity of this man is the deed which is indissolubly associated with his name—the building of the temple.

Why did he build that temple? I think in losing sight of the man's character we have missed the full significance of the deed. What was his motive for the erection of that stately pile? To fulfill a wish of his father? Partly. To satisfy a personal impulse of devotion? Partly. But I think neither of these standing alone nor both united would have impelled Solomon to such a work. Remember that this man was before all things a politician. David would have built the temple for "glory to God in the highest"; Solomon required the additional motive, "Peace on earth; goodwill among men."

What Solomon wanted above all things was a bond of national unity. Two rival ideals were dividing his empire—the house of David and the house of Saul. To the heart of Solomon there came the suggestion of a third and higher watchword—the house of God. Might not the two other houses be united in this wider building? Might not the memory of the long feud be made to perish in the common effort to inaugurate another kingdom, in the cooperation of both parties for the construction of a new and glorious palace—a palace compared to which the residence of a Saul and of a David would alike grow dim—a dwelling for the habitation of the King of Kings?

THE IDEA OF COMMON COOPERATION

Can you fail to see how in the building of this temple the idea of common cooperation occupies so prominent a place? Why are so many invited to contribute gifts? Why are such numbers solicited to lend a hand? Why is the work divided and subdivided between so many classes of laborers? Why is there a place for those who bear and a place for those who hew and a place for those who chip? Why is there such an enormous number of workmen as a hundred and eighty-three thousand and six hundred in a work protracted over seven years? Can there be any answer but one?

Do we not see that Solomon wants to be engaged in a work which will be the work of the nation—of the whole nation in all its parts and in all its members? He wants his people to be able to say not only, "Solomon did it," but, "We all did it with Solomon." He desires that every representative of Jewish life shall have a stone in the building.

The children shall bring their gifts to it; the adults shall bring their hands to it; the aged shall bring their prayers to it. The rich shall adorn it with gems; the poor shall serve it with their workmanship. The men of action shall break stones for it; the men of patience shall carry burdens for it; the men of taste shall contribute decorations for it. The poets shall make its songs; the musicians shall weave its memories; the theologians shall form its ritual.

That is the hope of Solomon—the dream of repiecing the rent garment. It is the hope that the tribe of Judah and the tribe of Benjamin may become tributaries to the river of God, that the wars sown in a divided empire may be forgotten in a united worship, and that the house of Saul may be joined to the house of David by that mysterious secret passage which runs through the house of the Lord.

A PRAYER

Lord, You are building a temple greater than that of Solomon— the temple of the Holy Ghost. Give me a stone in the building of that house! Give me a place in the work, suited to my soul. If I have many places in my soul, give me many duties for the temple. In my time of singing, train me for its choir. In my time of business, enrich me for its maintenance. In my time of health, strengthen me to raise its walls. In my time of sickness, give me patience to bear its burdens.

I would bring all my possessions of body and mind as subscriptions to the building. I bring You my gladness for its morning hymn. I bring You my sadness for its evening song. I bring You my beauty for its adorning. I bring You my defects for its altar of sacrifice. I bring You my strength that I may support some part; I bring You my weakness that some part may support me. I bring You my moments of faith that there may be service by day; I bring You my moments of doubt that there may be service by night. I bring You my full cup for the hour of thanksgiving; I bring You my empty cup for the hour of prayer.

Let all the gates of Your temple be open to my soul, O Lord; for I know not, in life's revolving, before what portal I may need to stand.

For Further Study and Reflection

1. Why did Israel desperately need a wise leader after David's reign? Compare David and Solomon.

2. Define true power. How did Solomon secure his throne?

3. What specifically did Solomon attain through his marriages? through his commerce? through building the Temple?

4. Why did Solomon encourage such wide participation by the people in the building of the temple?

5. Why is Solomon, above all, a politician?

3

ELIJAH THE IMPULSIVE

There are three men whom the Bible Gallery dissociates from
the idea of death—Enoch, Moses, and Elijah. Of each of
these it is virtually declared that no one can picture for them a
burying-place. Enoch has left no record of a closing life; Moses
has left no trace of a physical decay; Elijah has left no sign of an
extinguished fire. It is not, I think, by accident that the Great
Gallery has dissociated these three forms from the idea of the
dark valley.

These three forms represent three qualities which have no
historical limit, which are found side-by-side in every age—the
spirit, the conscience, and the heart. Enoch represents the spirit—
the craving for divine communion. Moses represents the
conscience—the eternal law of human duty. Elijah represents
the heart—the power that acts from the impulse of the moment.

These three phases of mind cannot be localized; they are historically immortal. We cannot say that spirituality belongs to
one century, conscience to another, impulse to a third. We cannot even say that within the memory of civilized man these three
have developed. Spinoza is not in advance of Plato; Paul is not
morally the superior of Moses; Luther is not more intense than
Simon Peter. In all ages of civilized time man has exhibited
equally these three phases—the spiritual, the moral, and the in-
tuitive. They have been, within this limit, not only deathless, but
seemingly changeless. The Gallery has proclaimed their immortality. It has incarnated each in the person of a separate life, and

then it has shown us that life standing apart from the elements of decay. Enoch has no tomb; Moses has no shroud; Elijah has no setting to the chariot of his sun.

NO RECORD OF DEATH

There is nothing which localizes a man like the record of his death. When you announce the date of a man's death, you fix the limit of his personal development in the present world. When you announce the date of his marriage or the date of his first publication, you give no clue to his ultimate mental standpoint. But the inscription on the tombstone is the latest possible record concerning the man; it stamps indelibly his century upon him; it marks the final stretch of his environment.

Here lies the significance of this record of the Gallery. When it shows us Enoch translated, when it conceals the body of Moses, when it reveals Elijah ascending in his chariot of fire, it virtually says, "Do not regard these men as belonging to a particular century. Look at them as symbolizing those three phases of the human mind which are the same in all centuries. View them as embodiments of the fact that there are three permanent elements in humanity—the devotional, the moral, and the instinctive. Consider them as revealers of the truth that, whatever else may faint or grow weary, these three will never die—the breathings of the spirit, the commands of the conscience, and the impulses of the heart."

ELIJAH THE MAN OF IMPULSE

I have attributed to Elijah the third of these positions. I regard him as distinctively the man of impulse, the man who is prompted by instinctive dictates. His life is one of sudden movements, of surprises. He is more like a lance than a sword. He does not fence, he darts. He breaks forth suddenly from the silence—and as suddenly vanishes.

Everything about him is abrupt; his beginning and his ending are abrupt. He comes without introduction, and he goes without warning. He appears before us like Melchizedek—without father or mother or descent. We see no childhood. We discover no home. We recognize no domestic interest. He comes before us as the Christ of St. Mark comes before us—full-grown, developed, equipped for his mission. He stands forth all at once in the political arena. In a moment, in the twinkling of an eye, we are confronted by a spectral form denouncing idolatry, predicting vengeance.

Not in the valley does he first appear. We see no trace of one who needs to climb. When we earliest meet him, it is at the top of the hill. He hurls his rebuke right at the throne. Reformers as a rule begin with the masses and creep up gradually to the classes. Elijah begins at the social summit. He stands in the court of Ahab, in the court of Jezebel; our first vision of him is in the presence of kings. He bursts upon us in full meridian.

There is no gradation between the depth of silence and the blare of trumpets—yesterday he was voiceless; today he is thunder. It is written of John the Baptist, "He was in the desert till the day of his showing unto Israel" (Luke 1:80). That could be written of Elijah. His development is quite hid from us. There is no boundary line between his desert and his glory. We do not see him rise; we behold him risen. A few minutes ago there was darkness all round; suddenly we are in the presence of a great fire whose kindling has been invisible to us, and whose origin we do not know.

It is my opinion that the history of Elijah, as recorded in the Great Gallery, is the history of all impulsive minds. The course of all such minds is a process not of increasing but of subsiding flame. I do not mean that they ever diminish the actual amount of their heat, but they diminish the amount of their heat in any one direction. All impulse is at first one-sided. It sees only a single way—the drastic way. It looks at the barren fig tree and says, "Cut it down; why cumbereth it the ground."

Later, the impulsive mind loses its haste—not from declining zeal but from increasing vision. It sees that there are other ways of dealing with the fig tree—that zeal may be intense without being drastic. This is the course of Elijah—a gradual subsiding from the roar into the whisper. It is a voice growing softer, becoming ever more calm—not because the heat has lost its passion, not because the soul has drooped its wing, but because the eye has seen more clearly the hope of ultimate success.

THE FIRST PHASE OF ELIJAH'S MINISTRY

Let us examine this process in the life of Elijah—this gradual subsiding of noise. He begins most vociferously. Like John the

Baptist, he comes out of his desert and shouts, "Repent!" His motive, however, is different from that of the Baptist. The Baptist denounced loose living; Elijah denounces idolatry. Elijah is more allied to John Knox who stood before Queen Mary than to the John who stood before King Herod. To John Knox, indeed, he presents a strong parallel.

Elijah, like Knox, is the child of a Protestant reaction. He appears as the champion of a faith which he believes to be the primitive faith—the worship of an invisible God. Men had sought to worship God in a material form, to see Him enshrined in some object of human sense. Elijah calls them to come back— back to the forest primeval, back to those grounds of Eden where God was distinct from the trees of the Garden.

Elijah is the uncompromising Protestant of his time, an opponent of the image in the sanctuary. But his weapons as yet are purely physical. He brings no arguments; he exhibits no reasons. The message he delivers is a menace, "Abandon your idols or die!" He recognizes but one force—outward compulsion. "You have bowed down to idols; you will have drought and famine!"—that is the burden of his message. There is no appeal to philosophy; there is no invitation to a controversy; there is no attempt to exhibit the inherent nature of the sin. There is simply a call to arms—a command to extirpate those who revered the forms of nature.

Elijah, then, displays at the outset the full amount of his fire— his fire concentrated on a single point. The problem is how to get that fire distributed. We do not wish to see it extinguished; we do not even wish to see it reduced; we want to see it diffused, spread in different directions, made less one-sided. The effect of all one-sided emotion is a collapse of the man who feels it. It is so with Elijah.

ELIJAH'S EXHAUSTION

Where do we next meet with him? In a desert place by the side of the brook Cherith. What has brought him there? "The fear of King Ahab," says the Bible student. I do not believe it. Has he not just been in the presence of Ahab, defying him to the face, denouncing his idolatry, proclaiming his retribution? If Elijah had been a timid man, then was the time for fear. Could you imagine a man who braved Ahab to his face running off in terror when Ahab had turned his back? No—not in terror. But I could imagine him doing so in physical prostration. In fact, no other explanation can be given.

Why should this brave, bold man who had met the hour of danger with unblanched cheek be found, when the crisis was past, lurking in a desolate spot by the brook Cherith? It can only be accounted for by nerve-exhaustion—by the process of reaction from strong emotion. Elijah at the brook Cherith is an illustration of that principle which has ruled in all minds of one-sided impulse. If he had been divided between anger and sorrow and pity, he would have experienced no mental reaction; the alternations of feeling would have saved him from collapse. But he abandoned himself to a single impulse, and the inevitable result was the prostration at the waters of Cherith.

ELIJAH'S FIRST LESSON

And now I have to observe that this reaction was the finest training which the man could possibly have received. It gave him his first lesson in something he had much need to learn— the superiority of mental force to material force. He had been conquering Ahab by physical strength; but immediately afterwards he is himself conquered by a silently working influence— a power impalpable to sense, independent of weapons. He has been prostrated by a process working quicker than famine, quicker than drought, quicker than pestilence; he has been prostrated by the very sweep of his own mental energy.

Was not this a message to his soul? He had mistaken the comparative strength of the natural forces. Did it not say to him that he had chosen the least powerful agency when he selected drought and famine as the ministers of God? Did it not tell him that he should have appealed to the mind of Ahab, that he should have tried to exhibit rather the inner than the outer majesty of God? Elijah was to be taught that the best cure for idolatry was not the exhibition of the divine hand but the exhibition of the divine heart. God was better than the idol not because He could break the idol but because He could give what the idol could not—help in the day of trouble.

Elijah, then, must be taught that the highest glory of true

religion, and what distinguishes it from false religion, is its power to minister. And this, by the brook Cherith, is God's lesson to his soul.

GOD'S MESSAGE TO ELIJAH'S SOUL

The ravens unconsciously bring him food. Unable in the famine to find grain, they bear to the spot the bodies of animals which they have slain and deposit them there for their future use. Elijah inherits the fruit of their labors. He appropriates the spoil they have gathered. but he regards them as his unconscious almsgivers. Yet, his countrymen had always deemed the raven an unholy thing. It was ill omened. The lamb, the dove, and the goat were objects of divine association; the raven was not. Men did not present it in sacrifice.

But here God presents the raven in sacrifice. God tells Elijah to receive it as His minister. And then there comes a strange call to Elijah which perhaps I may be allowed to paraphrase: "Elijah, there are better modes of teaching My service than breaking and bruising. You have been ministered unto by creatures which you deem unholy; will not you minister unto such? If I can make sacrilegious things My instruments, shall you be afraid to touch them? Will you not best conquer them by showing them the beauty of holiness? Come, and I will tell you how to show the beauty of holiness to one of those whom you call sacrilegious.

"There is a widow in great want in the country of Tyre and Sidon. She is beyond the boundaries of your land. She belongs to a heathen population. She worships Me not after the pattern of your fathers. But she has a body of like passions with you. She has felt the hunger which you have felt—the hunger which the ravens have fed. Go, and minister to her as the ravens have ministered to you. You will reveal to her the power of your God more clearly by that deed than by all the storms of denunciation and all the instruments of destruction."

The aim of this call is to broaden Elijah—to lead him to the belief that the absence of true religion is not so much something to be punished with famine as something which proves famine to be already there. He is to be made to feel that the man or woman so afflicted is primarily an object not of anger but of pity. He is to be led to realize that the subjects of this malady are experiencing a sense of want and therefore are objects of charity rather than marks for vengeance.

Each Stage In Elijah's Life Is a Humbling Stage

That is the reason why every stage of Elijah's course is a humbling stage. He is constantly met by some privation; every morning of hope is followed by a night of despair. Why so? we are inclined to ask; why should God obstruct the missionary work of His servant? Simply because the obstruction of the work is in his case the advancement of the man. What he needs to know above all things is the sense of want—the sympathy with human weakness.

He has been born with too much independence in his heart. His native instinct is towards self-reliance. What he deems easy he thinks everybody should deem easy. The lesson he needs from life is an experience of individual feebleness.

Elijah is the natural opposite of David. David had conflicting currents in him, and therefore he felt weak; Elijah had originally only one current, and therefore he felt strong. The aim of the Almighty is to send new currents through him and so to make him feel more conflict. He is not humanitarian enough, because he is not near enough to the ground. He does not make allowance for human frailty, because he is too confident of himself. He must be taught self-distrust that he may learn the needs of mankind. The greatest convert made by Elijah's mission was to be—Elijah.

Elijah on Mount Carmel

Not all at once did this conversion come; it was gradual. When next the curtain rises, he is already in some measure liberalized. He consents to meet the idolaters at an ecumenical council on Mount Carmel. That was a large concession from a man of his uncompromising spirit. This was not the method in which he had first met Ahab. Then he had allowed no discussion; he had simply said, "Accept the doctrine or receive the scourge!" Now it is otherwise.

Elijah proposes a test of truth, a mental test—the comparative power of prayer. Let us try, he says, which of our prayers will impart most fire to life! That was a fair field of battle; what can be a better test of religion than its power to impart vital fire?

It was a field on which Elijah was sure to win. No unspiritual worship is ever kindling; love alone can illuminate the common way. Elijah triumphed in the argument; he showed what on his side had been wrought by prayer. It would have been well had he rested with that victory. But the militant instinct was not dead within him. The meeting closed in bloodshed. What happened I do not exactly know; the picture in the Gallery leaves something to the imagination.

I suppose that Elijah, heated by his new kind of triumph, harangued the crowd and rhetorically called upon his countrymen to root out from among them these corrupters of the national faith. I suppose that the crowd, mistaking rhetoric for prose and interpreting the exhortation to extirpate a principle as the command to slay its adherents, rushed frantically and tumultuously on the prophets of Baal and gave them the crown of martyrdom. That Elijah designed the deed, I do not believe; that he regretted it, I firmly hold. Yet it was the fruit of his one-sided passion, and it brought a dark night to close a bright day.

ELIJAH'S FLIGHT

The martyrdom he had given to Baal was indeed a crown; violence always helps the cause on which it tramples. The clamors of the land rose against Elijah. To a man conscious of the justice of his deed this would have been little; but Elijah's inner man rose against himself. The prophet of God fled. From whom did he flee? Was it from Ahab? Was it from Jezebel? Was it from the friends of the martyred men of Baal? No; it was from his own inner man.

Elijah saw his other self—the self that was bound for heaven. It was as yet only a child, but it made him tremble. It shook his nerves; it paralyzed his self-confidence. He ran to escape the child, but the child ran with him; the child was his angel sent from God. He ran to Beersheba; he found the child at Beersheba. He fled into the Arabian desert; he met the child there. He lay down to die under a juniper tree; the child sustained him. He came to Horeb and hid himself in a mountain cave; the child suddenly became full grown, and Elijah recognized his true self.

ELIJAH'S VISION

For now there bursts upon his view a wondrous vision—the vision of his own life; and in a moment, in the twinkling of an eye, he finds that he has been on the wrong way. He hears a roaring wind; he says, "Is it You, Lord?" —there is no answer. He feels a trembling of the earth; he says, "Is it You, Lord?"— there is no answer. He sees a ball of fire shot into the air; he says, "Is it You, Lord?"—there is no answer. He catches the sound of a still, small voice, so low that he can hardly detect it; he says, "Is it You, Lord?"—and the answer comes, "It is I."

Could anything more completely reveal the plan of the Gallery in delineating the figure of Elijah? The design is popularly thought to be the exhibition of a physical heroism. It is the reverse. It is the exhibition of a process by which a great soul was made meet for heaven by altering its ideal of heroism from the physical to the mental.

The plan of the picture is to reveal a work of transition—a work in which the original mountain became a valley and the original valley became a mountain. In the cave of Horeb the transition was complete. The old Elijah was buried there, and the new Elijah emerged full grown. The child had conquered the man and left his body in the cave; the still, small voice had triumphed over the wind, the earthquake, and the fire.

THE CHANGE IN ELIJAH

Henceforth I see a change in Elijah. His alternations of hope and despair have vanished, and in their room there has come an equable calm. He is more trustful in adversity; he is more merciful in prosperity. His later denunciations are rather against inhumanity to mankind than against errors in creed or ritual. He avenges, and rightly avenges, the wrongs of Naboth; but, for the first time in the record of his life, his vengeance is mixed with leniency—a leniency all the more remarkable because it was exercised towards his consistent and inveterate enemy, Ahab.

No one can resist the conclusion that the Elijah who emerges from the cave of Horeb is an altered being. He is no longer a flaming sword; he is a human voice—wakened by human sympathies, tuned by human feelings. He has been made more fit to

meet Moses on the Mount; the power of action has been joined
to the power of waiting.

The working of this change was doubtless mainly from
within. But it was not wholly so. That voice in the cave of
Horeb said many things; but it said one thing which was
specially helpful to the future development of Elijah—it directed
him where to find a human friend. If there was one thing Elijah
needed to mellow him, it was that! He seems never to have felt
the influence of home ties. We read of no brother or sister; we
hear of no wife or child. His life throughout had been one of
war, of public commotion, of political and religious strife.
Superiors he had, inferiors he had; but, so far as I know, he had
hitherto possessed no equals. There had been no comrade of
his heart, no companion of his soul, none to take his hand and
say, "We are brothers."

A man in such a position is in want of one-half of life's
music. Was it not well to send him the friend Elisha? When the
voice sent him to Elisha, it sent him to a new school—a school
in which he would meet a kindred mind and experience at the
last those ties of human sympathy to which the days of his
actual childhood had been strangers. There, in the companion-
ship of Elisha, we will for the present leave him—ripening for a
higher destiny and preparing for enrollment in a loftier band
than the prophets of ancient Israel.

A PRAYER

I thank You, O Lord, that to Elijah and to me You have
revealed a new and better way. I thank You that the still, small
voice has taken the place of the wind, the earthquake, and the
fire. I used to think that law would redeem Your world. I thought
that stern penalties would repress the course of crime, that the
thunders of Sinai would make the sinner pure. I thought the
vision of the lake that burneth with fire and brimstone would put
out the love of evil.

You have taught me better, O my Father! You have taught me
that the love of evil can only be extinguished by another love.
My heart cannot be conquered by the hand. If it is centered on
the Prince of Evil, it will not be cured by the imprisonment of
that prince; I should love him in his prison, I should love him in

his bonds. If I am to cease loving him, I must have a new prince—the Prince of Peace.

Send me this new Prince, O my Father; nothing but Christ will put out Barabbas from my heart! I love wrongly, but none the less do I love intensely; nothing but another love will set me free. Famine will not; Carmel will not; wind and earthquake and fire will not; the burning lake itself would not extinguish my love.

Therefore, my Father, let me love again, let me love anew! Send into my heart a fresh ideal. Send me a sight of the "Altogether Lovely." Send me a vision of the "Chief Among Ten Thousand." Send me a picture of Him who is "fairer than the children of men." Break the old ideal by the vision of a higher beauty. Let my night fade in Your morning, my thorn vanish in Your flower! One leaf of Your summer's bloom will disenchant me of the winter's charm. The idols will be "broken in the temple of Baal" when I see Your King "on the holy hill of Zion."

For Further Study and Reflection

1. What is sudden about Elijah's appearance in Scripture? What is significant about having no record of his death?

2. Why did God's use of a raven to minister to Elijah have special significance?

3. Why does Elijah need to learn sympathy with human weakness?

4. How are Elijah's denunciations after his time in the cave at Horeb different from his earlier denunciations?

5. Why did Elijah need a human friend?

4

ELISHA THE IMITATIVE

As I pause before the figure of Elisha, perhaps the thought suggested to a bystander will be, Why do you make this a representative man? Is not the most distinctive feature about him just his want of originality? Is he not almost a direct copy of the form and face of Elijah? If there were no name inscribed below the picture, shouldn't we deem it simply a second likeness by an inferior hand? If so, why linger over the second delineation? We have seen the fire in the eye of the master; why pause to describe in the disciple the same eye without the fire? Should we not be better employed if we passed to fresh woods and pastures new?

PARALLELS BETWEEN ELIJAH AND ELISHA

Let me admit at once that the parallel is striking—far too striking to be the result of accident or unconscious workmanship. Elijah and Elisha are twin figures—what the one does, the other does. Their lives are set to the same music; the latter is the refrain of the former sung by a weaker voice and tuned to a slower measure. Does Elijah smite the waters of Jordan? Elisha does so too. Does Elijah ascend Mount Carmel? Elisha does so too. Do the words of Elijah cause a bloody tragedy? The words of Elisha do so too. Is Elijah appealed to in times of drought? Elisha is so too. Does Elijah multiply a widow's store? Elisha does so too. Does Elijah raise a widow's son? Elisha raises one too. Does Elijah carry his beneficence beyond the confines of Judaism? Elisha does so too—if the one ministers to a woman of

Zarephath, the other cures the captain of a Syrian band. Finally, does Elijah in his last earthly moments hear the triumphant cry, "The chariots of Israel and the horsemen thereof"? Elisha in his last earthly moments listens to the same sound and experiences at the hour of death what his master had experienced at the hour of ascension.

A UNIQUE PICTURE OF FELLOWSHIP

If, then, I admit this remarkable parallel, if I regard Elisha as a designed imitation of Elijah, why do I not pass him by as a repetition of old material? It is because this imitation of character is itself in the Old Testament Gallery a new and unique thing. I do not know whether it has occurred to anyone that the relation of Elisha to Elijah supplies a desired essential in the Gallery.

Among the figures of this collection I look in vain for any evidence of that community of mind which in the New Testament is called fellowship. Up to this point we have not found in these studies two men who have been united by similarity of spirit. The one has rather been the complement of the other, has supplied what was lacking in the other. Isaac has little likeness to Abraham; Joseph moves in a different sphere from Jacob; Solomon has few points in common with David. Joshua may be called the disciple of Moses, but only in a figurative sense. He is more a servant than a son; he carries out his orders, but he does not stand with him on the Mount.

The truth is, kindred sympathy is a very rare thing to get. Personal liking—the feeling that existed between David and Jonathan—is very easily acquired; but the congruity of thought, the identity of experience, which made the bond between Elisha and Elijah—that is something which is never acquired at all; the germ of it must be born in each soul. To exhibit this double portion of one experience is a work which may well absorb the interest of the religious artist. This, then, is a case of intellectual friendship which is unique in the Old Testament Gallery.

ELISHA IS LIKE THE SECOND ELIJAH

I have said that in germ Elisha must have had from birth the spirit of Elijah. But the question occurs, To which of the Elijahs was he allied? We have seen that there were two—that one died in the cave of Horeb and that the other came out of the cave full grown. Elisha never saw the first; his personal contact was with the second. The second Elijah, the Elijah who emerged from the cave, was of a gentler nature than the first; he had abandoned the wind, the earthquake, and the fire for the still, small voice.

Elisha was by nature allied to this later Elijah. God had given him a tender heart, a heart of love. When first we meet with him, it is in the circle of family life; and we have evidence that his ties of home were dear. Elijah finds him at the plow and calls him to quit the world for the prophetic sanctuary. He asks to be allowed to bid his father and mother good-bye. And that good-bye is a fine revelation of character.

Elisha makes a feast to his old friends. He wants them to understand that he has not parted with them in anger, has not left the world because the grapes are sour or the vintage bad. When a man is going abroad, we often give him a parting dinner to wish him well. But if a man going abroad gives us a parting dinner, the act has a still deeper significance. It says that however prosperous he may be in the new country, he wishes it to be understood that the old land will still be dear to his heart. He says, in effect, I do not leave you through disgust; I do not quit you through disapproval; I do not say that it is bad for you to remain; I part from your world not in a blast of anger but in a flood of joyous memories which, even while it bears me away, repeats the echoes from my native shore.

ELISHA'S WARM, EARTHLY FRIENDSHIP

Elisha, then, even in the hour of his election, is no ascetic. He brings to Elijah a human heart. It was the latest and the best gift Elijah had ever received—a pure earthly friendship. Elisha gave him his heart, his whole heart, his unrestrained heart. I cannot too strongly emphasize this point; it is something unique in the Old Gallery. Men had hitherto come to God through a crucifixion of their human nature. They had approached Mount Sinai with fear and trembling; they had drawn near the burning bush with uncovered feet. But Elisha comes unshorn of his humanity. He comes to the Divine Presence in the dress of a man, with the heart of a man. He is drawn to the heavenly Father by the love of an earthly brother.

Elisha is not ashamed, from the very outset, to lean upon a

human arm. This utilizing of earthly help remains his characteristic through life; it colors every sphere through which he moves. I will take four of these spheres—the moral, the intellectual, the aesthetic, and the practical. We shall find in each abundant material for reflection and abundant sources of suggestion.

ELISHA'S MORAL CHOICE

The first illustration of Elisha's tendency to use secular, earthly help is in his moral choice. His master, Elijah, has a premonition of his own early removal. He asks the disciple what mark of his favor he would like best to receive as a parting gift. Elisha answers, "Let a double portion of thy spirit be upon me" (2 Kings 2:9). By "a double portion" I understand "a repeated portion—a repetition of your own experience." It is the request for a token of human love.

Elisha does not wish the grace of God to be for him a supernatural thing. He wants to be like someone whom he loves and whom he loves on account of his goodness. Is not Christianity the selfsame prayer on a higher plane? Is it not simply the wish that in our hearts the grace of God would assume the likeness of one whom we love—the Man Christ Jesus? Like Elisha, we cannot worship an abstract grace. We must see it embodied if we are to love it. Our desire to be clothed in it must be the desire to be clothed in the likeness of one who was dear to us. St. John was animated by a human love of Jesus; therefore he does not say, "When He shall appear we shall be good," but, "When He shall appear we shall be like Him" (1 John 3:2).

ELISHA'S REQUEST FOR A TOKEN OF LOVE

That Elisha's aspiration was the request for a token of love is confirmed by Elijah's answer, "Thou hast asked a great thing; nevertheless, if thou see me when I am taken from thee, it will be so unto thee; if not, it shall not be so" (2 Kings 2:10). He says that whether his disciple's desire be or be not granted is a question that can only be tested by Elisha's future remembrance.

Separated from the figurative envelope which contains them, his words amount to this: "The test of a kindred spirit is sight in absence. Can you sustain that test? Can you see me when I am taken up? Can you feel the power of my presence when that presence is no longer with you? Can you be impelled by my influence when I have withdrawn my hand? Can I be a motive to your life when I have ceased to be in touch with it? If so, then you have indeed received into your soul a duplicate of my image. You have proved your possession of a kindred nature; you have maintained your right to wear my mantle."

Remember that the test proposed by Elijah is also the test proposed by a greater than Elijah. What else does Christ mean by the parable of a man going into a far country and bidding his servants work till his return? It is to ascertain whether they are fit for the mantle, whether they have received his spirit. The test of that will be their power to think of his presence in his absence, to feel as if he were near when he is far away.

THE EVIDENCE THAT THE MANTLE HAS DESCENDED

The evidence of the disciple's communion with Christ is identical with Elisha's evidence for his communion with Elijah; it is the "seeing him who is invisible," the bending to an influence which is not manifested either to the eye or to the ear or to the hand. Elisha saw Elijah after he was taken up; the disciples worshiped Jesus after the cloud had received Him out of their sight; in both cases it was an evidence that the mantle had descended.

Elisha, then, was helped to the grace of God by a human love, and that human love abode with him long after its object had been hid from his outward sight. It is the first instance of the kind we have met with in the Great Gallery, but it has been the forerunner of many similar experiences. There are hundreds whose belief in God sprang at first from belief in man. There are hundreds who have given their allegiance to the Divine by fixing their eye upon some beauty in the human. There are hundreds who, like Elisha, have served the God whom they have not seen simply because they have loved the brother whom they have seen.

This old painting is not obsolete, not dead. It is living, breathing, vitalizing. It is mirrored in myriad lives; it is reproduced in countless experiences; it is a picture which is neither Jewish nor Greek nor Roman but human. It expresses not the bias of a nation but an instinct of the heart; and therefore its colors are not dimmed by time—they are as fresh and vivid today as they were in the streets of ancient Israel.

ELISHA'S INTELLECTUAL ATTITUDE

The second illustration of Elisha's secular, earthly attitude will be found in the intellectual sphere. He has been left alone; the master whom he loved has passed into the silent land. Elisha has no doubt that Elijah has been translated into heaven; he is as sure of that as he is of his own existence.

But Elisha is a professor in a college. He has the Chair of Apologetics and is the director of what was then called "The School of the Prophets." He has a host of young men who listen to his instructions and for whose training he is responsible. These young men are tinged with the spirit of a new age—an age of rationalism. They are very unwilling to admit a miracle. They are eager to reduce everything to natural causes.

They propose to subject the belief in Elijah's ascension to scientific experts. They suggest that his chariot may have been one of the wild blasts of the desert. Instead of being taken to heaven, he may have been carried to the summit of some hill where he may be lying bruised and broken. Will not Elisha allow a search to be made? Instead of cherishing a mystical exaltation, will he not let fifty strong men go forth in search of the vanished prophet? If they should find him, it would be the death of sentiment; but it might produce a result which would prove more valuable than any sentiment—the preservation of a physical life.

ELISHA'S WILLINGNESS TO SERVE HIS STUDENTS

At first Elisha said, "No"; but afterwards he said, "Yes." That saying "Yes" is to my mind one of the finest things in old literature. Why does he say "Yes"? Is it because he has any doubt of the truth of his first impression? He has no doubt. But he has cast himself down from his own pinnacle; he has put himself in the place of his students; he has tried to live in the experience of those who have less strong faith than himself. He feels that he has Elijah for his model. Did not Elijah hold a council for research on Mount Carmel—Elijah who needed no investigation, no argument? Should the disciple be above his master? Might not he, Elisha, do what was virtually done by the prophet of fire? If his master could sink himself to help idolaters, might not he sink himself for the sake of his own students? Should he not go down to them who were as yet unable to come up to him?

Now, I say this was grand in Elisha. If all his prophetic powers should come to be ignored, he ought to live by this deed alone. It was the best lesson he ever gave to his students—this accommodation to their intellectual need. It is a lesson for professors as well as students. I would say to a teacher: Never force your certainty upon your pupil. Borrowed convictions are of no value. Command not assent to former testimonies—not even to the authority of your own vision. Let the pupil search for Elijah. Let him seek him on every hill; let him inquire for his steps in every valley. Lend him all facilities for the search. Open every avenue; unlock every gate; clear every barrier that would impede his way. At the end of many days he may reach by climbing the height which you have gained by a moment on the wing.

ELISHA'S USE OF ESTHETICS

The third of those spheres in which Elisha leans upon material help in the things of divine grace is the esthetic region—the attempt to exhibit the beauties of holiness. Elisha has gone to meet three kings. It is a period of political emergency, and they have summoned him into their presence to ask his counsel. Elisha is impressed with the august character of his audience. He wishes to speak well. He is not only desirous to do his duty in the sight of God but to magnify his office in the sight of man.

He has the feeling which belongs to every popular preacher— the wish to produce an esthetic effect upon his hearers. It is a feeling which is quite compatible with the most earnest religious devotion. Accordingly, he wishes to rise to the occasion. In order to do so, he would like the aid of a stimulus. The stimulus he selects is music. "Bring me a minstrel," he says (2 Kings 3:15). He feels that he would speak better if he has a pleasant environment; he evokes the aid of nature to help him in the sphere of grace.

Now, this is a very startling thing. We all admit the power of natural beauty in the region of natural work. That a poet is helped by a sunbeam, that a literary style is influenced by fair surroundings, that imagination is stimulated by a starry night or quickened by a mountain view—all this is universally accepted.

But in the sphere of grace we are apt to think such helps superfluous. We are apt to believe that the Spirit of God is a solitary agent acting by its own strength and conquering by its own power. We think of the beauties of holiness as themselves sufficient to inspire. Shall the heavenly manna seek an ally in the earthly music? Shall the hand of God work in unison with the harp of man? Shall the soul be aided to its vision of divine glory by listening to the strains of a purely human melody and thrilling to the notes of an instrument with mundane strings?

Elisha says, "Yes"; he calls for a minstrel before prophesying. The minstrel was probably a man vastly inferior to himself and was perhaps not a religious man at all, yet Elisha was not ashamed to use him for the service of God. Was he here again influenced by the memory of Elijah, by the tendency to imitate his master? Did he remember how that master was fed by ravens? Did he remember how the mightiest was supported by the ministration of the meanest? Did he remember how the mere secular forces of life had been made to serve the kingdom of God? I think it likely.

Elisha must have felt that if the tempestuous soul of his master could be content to be fed by earthly streams, the quiet river of his own life might well be thus satisfied too. At all events, he was content. He was satisfied to sun himself in a worldly beauty, to cheer himself into the work for God by a study of the work of man. In his moment of spiritual exhaustion he sought a secular stimulus. At a time when be had nothing to draw with, he let a Samaritan bring the pitcher. In the hour when his alabaster box was broken, he allowed his costliest treasures to be carried in earthen vessels.

THE CHRISTIAN CHURCH FOLLOWS ELISHA'S EXAMPLE

And the Christian church has followed the example of Elisha. The voice of that church has ever increasingly been, "Bring me a minstrel!" She began without the ministrel—in the humble precincts of an upper room. But she found that she needed stimulus. She was marching as an army to battle; and, like an army marching to battle, she required a blast of music. Christianity has ascended the hill to the tune of trumpets on the plain; the feet of the Christian soldier have moved in unison with the measure of an earthly melody.

The religion of the Cross has proceeded up the Dolorous Way crowned with the flowers of the world's field. It has availed itself

of every secular aid. It has beautified the places of its worship. It
has imparted human graces to its heavenly services. It has cultivated by natural art the voices of its choristers. It has sent its
prophets to drink at the wells of worldly wisdom. It has given a
literary form to its liturgies. It has incorporated with its psalmody
the sentiments of men not called inspired. When we see the Christian church ascending, we cry with Elisha, "The chariots of Israel
and the horsemen thereof" but we feel that the chariots and the
horsemen belong to different worlds—that the horsemen are of
heaven, the chariots of earth.

ELISHA'S USE OF THE PRACTICAL

I come now to the fourth of these spheres in which Elisha
allies himself to the earthly, the secular; it is the practical sphere—
the sphere of the physician. The incident to which I allude is the
healing of Naaman the Syrian.

Naaman is a leper, and he repairs to Elisha in the hope of a
cure. Elisha tells him to bathe seven times in the waters of the
Jordan. Naaman is incensed; he thinks the prophet has insulted
him. Why so? Myriads of sermons have been written on the
subject, and the prevailing note of all has been that Naaman was
offended by the simplicity of the proposed remedy. Do you think
that likely? If I go to a doctor expecting to be prescribed a
drastic operation, and if I am told instead simply to bathe in cold
water, am I not likely rather to congratulate myself than to feel
angry? Naaman himself says in the narrative that he would have
been content with something much more simple—a mere touch
of the prophet's hand.

The sting lay in the fact that the prophet himself took no part
in the cure. He handed Naaman over to the powers of nature—to
the waters of Jordan. Naaman wanted to be the subject of a
supernatural influence—to be directly favored by the emissary
of the God of Israel. That emissary, instead of calling in mysterious helps, instead of engaging in prayer or indulging in incanta-
tions, sent him to a bathing establishment and told him to continue
his attendance there until the cleansing process was complete.
Naaman very naturally felt that he might have found such institutions nearer home. The entire ground of his anger lay in the
knowledge that Elisha was not eager to be thought the agent in

the cure, that, instead of being proud to have so august a patient, he had calmly handed him over to the care of one of his assistant physicians—to the medical skill of the waters of Jordan.

What to Naaman was a source of anger is to us a source of satisfaction. We are glad that Elisha, when he sought the help of God, sought it through the channels of nature—that he claimed the secular forces as workers of the divine will. But I think that here, as elsewhere, Elisha was influenced by that personal memory which had been his constant guide.

Why does he send Naaman to the waters of Jordan? Was it not because these waters embodied the latest memory of him whom he loved—that memory which had imparted to Elisha himself a healing touch in every hour of weariness and had inspired him with fresh strength amid the burden and heat of the day? It was on the banks of the Jordan that he had gazed on Elijah almost for the last time; it was on the banks of the Jordan that he had seen his very last act of power. It was love's latest image in his soul.

In sending Naaman to the Jordan, Elisha felt that he was sending him to Elijah. He was putting him in hands that were mightier than his own. He was evoking the spirit of his departed friend to help his healing work—to be the sole agent in that work. He says, in effect, "I commit this man into your hands; you who have smitten the waters of the Jordan, smite upon these waters the leprosy of Naaman."

From first to last the spirit of Elijah had remained Elisha's guiding star. It had spoken to him from the silent land. He had dedicated everything to its memory, to its example. To that memory he dedicated the waters of the Jordan too. They were to him sparkling with the sunset of yesterday, and he sent the leper Naaman to be partaker of their beams.

A PRAYER

I thank You, O Father, that in the pictures of the Great Gallery there is a memorial to human friendship—to the love of two human souls. I thank You that You have suffered Elisha to be swayed by the memory of a departed friend; it is Your own image on the sacredness of earthly love. I thank You that You have allowed my heart to wear the mantle of the departed. You have not forced me to think of the chariots and horsemen that have borne him away. You have permitted me to picture my Elijah in the old scenes.

You have allowed me to figure him on the heights of Carmel and on the banks of the Jordan. You have allowed me to hear his footsteps on my earthly way—to be guided by his example, to be inspired by his remembrance. Why have You not bid me forget? Why have You not told Elisha to think of his own way and let his friend rest behind the veil? Why have You counseled him to look up and see if any mantle from his vanished friend is falling?

Is it not to tell him, to tell me, that love is eternal? Is it not to tell me that the chariot of fire cannot part human friendships? Is it not to tell me that the fire of death cannot burn up the mantle of earthly influence? Often in the vision of departing chariots I am complaining of the waste of life. I see men taken up before their work is done, and I weep for their unfinishedness. Teach me by this scene in the Great Gallery that Elijah can finish his work from beyond the grave. Teach me that the box of ointment is not wasted when it is broken. Teach me that the fragrance can fill the house when the fragments are on the floor. Teach me that a departed life may hold in my heart an empire which no present life can claim. So shall I learn the immortality of love.

For Further Study and Reflection

1. What are some examples of Elisha's warm and connected personality?

2. In what four spheres does Elisha use earthly, secular examples to teach his students and show God's ways?

3. Elisha needed Elijah's example and spirit when Elijah was gone. How do we need Christ's example even when Christ is in heaven?

4. Why must a student come to his own convictions and not merely those of his teacher?

5. How was sending Naaman to the Jordan for healing like sending him to the spirit of Elijah?

JOB THE PATIENT

The portrait of Job has been attributed to every date between the extremes of a thousand years—from the call of Abraham to the calling back of Judah's bondage. My own opinion is that it dates from the Persian period. I think that an artist of that day delineated the facts of a real historic tradition, but I believe that he used them to express an allegory. Job is to me not merely an individual; he is that, and he is something more.

Job is the personification of the Jewish race in captivity. Through the personality of Job the artist aims to show that the afflictions of his people ought not to be attributed to any special sin and that the exile they have been doomed to bear may itself have been a part of their mission from the Highest. The fact that when the portrait was being painted the national clouds were already beginning to be parted by streaks of sunshine may have lent inspiration to the thought. I turn, however, from the critical to the human.

I will view this not as the portrait of a nation but as the portrait of a man, and I will only consider in it those qualities which belong to the individual heart; Judah has passed away, but Job abides.

DESPAIR IN LITERATURE

There have been four typical notes of despair in the region of literature. The first and most intense is the voice of Omar Khayyam. It is despair absolute, despair of life all round, despair whose only relief is to drown itself in wine.

The second is the book of Ecclesiastes. I would call it despair of results. It does not deny that it is a pleasant thing to see the light of the sun; it does not dispute that there is a time to dance as well as a time to weep; but it asks, What is the good of it? Does it not all end in vanity?

The third is the cry of Pascal. It is despair of everything finite—finite reason, finite love, finite pleasure; the only possible joy is joy in God.

The fourth is that dramatic portraiture which we call the book of Job. I would describe it as the despair of old theories. It is the least despondent of the group. It does not say that the world is bad; it does not say that life is vanity; it does not even say that finite things cannot bring joy. What it does say is that all the past theories to explain the evils of the universe have been utterly powerless to account for these evils, that none of them is fit to sustain the weight of human woes, and that all of them put together are inadequate to wipe the tear from a single eye.

The book of Job is not strictly a pessimistic book. It does not despair of the universe—in spite of all its sorrows! What it does despair of is the adequacy of any one of man's existing theories, or of all these theories united, to furnish a solution of its sorrows. It does not deny that there may be summer somewhere beyond the sea, but it refuses to accept the doctrine that any of the previous swallows have ever touched the gilded shore.

A New Theory of the Origin of Pain

Now, observe carefully why the book of Job rejects old theories of the origin of pain. It is because it has found a new theory. All the former ones had explained suffering as the result of defect in the creature. Here the bold view is advanced that it had its origin in a need felt by the Creator—the divine need for love. With startling originality and for the first time in history, this book declares that the pains of earth were born in heaven, that they originated in the counsels beyond the veil.

Let us stand before this picture in the Great Gallery; it is one of the most striking not only in all Scripture but in all literature. It reveals in the foreground a day in heaven. It is a great day—a day of presentations. All quarters of the universe are represented. Each has sent up a deputy to stand before the throne of God.

Looking round the vast assembly, the eye of the Almighty lights upon a strange figure; it is that of Satan.

"Where do you come from?" says the Almighty. "What part of the universe has made you its representative?"

Satan answers, "I represent the earth—the length of it, the breadth of it."

"Not in its whole extent," says the Almighty. "There is a man called Job down in the land of Uz who loves Me fervently."

DIVINE LOVE ASSOCIATED WITH TEMPORAL REWARDS

"Oh!" cries Satan, "nobody loves you for yourself—not even Job! You have made it worthwhile to serve You. You have given to those who obey you houses and brethren and lands. You have crowned them with glory and honor; you have promised them long life and prosperity. Take away from Job the dowry he gets for loving You—take away the rich possessions that have rewarded his fidelity, and he will curse You to Your face!"

The Almighty accepts this criticism. Satan has put his hand upon a real weakness of the Hebrew race—its association of divine love with temporal rewards. God tells Satan to go forth and create a set of new conditions—conditions unfavorable to man's love of the Divine. He bids him put this man Job under a testing probation—a probation in which he will be denuded of every outward joy and made to experience the fact that a man may serve the Lord and get nothing in return.

JOB'S MISSION IS SIMPLY TO BEAR

So Satan goes out from the presence of the Lord, and in the changing of Job's environment he constructs a unique figure in the Old Testament Gallery—a figure which has the stamp of a distinctively new conception. Job is the only man of the Old Gallery whose mission is simply to bear.

All the other men of the group are men of action. Enoch had the breath of immortality, but Enoch's life was a walk with God. Elijah had a chariot of fire, but Elijah was the prophet of fire. Noah rose above the floods of fortune, but Noah was an active shipbuilder. Abraham was highly blessed, but Abraham was the founder of a kingdom. Moses communed with God on the Mount as a man talks with his friend, but Moses was the maker of practical laws. All these were great by reason of their working.

But this man Job comes upon the scene to do nothing—simply to bear. To the eye of the beholder it does not appear that the bearing has any practical purpose. He is not weighted, as Isaac was, with the cares of a household. He is weighted seemingly for the sake of nobody, but just with a view to his own pain. What we see is a process of divestiture—and the reason is known only to the spectator. He comes to be dismantled. One by one the beautiful robes are taken off until every thread of former majesty is gone, until the king becomes a pauper and the millionaire a beggar for bread. Let us follow the process.

JOB'S DIVESTITURE

First the outermost robe is removed—worldly wealth takes wings and vanishes away; the labor of the olive fails and the field supplies no meat. Job stands the test; his love for God wavers not.

Then an inner robe is removed—the ties of home are broken by death. His had been a happy domestic circle—a circle of family reunions. They met at these reunions once a year in the rotation of each son's birthday. We all know the increasing sadness of these gatherings—the sadness of hearing voices that are no longer there. Job had to bear this. Year by year the vacant chairs increased in prominence, and the touch of vanished hands became more frequent. Still he wavers not; no cry escapes his lips.

Then a more inward robe still is taken—health breaks; bodily strength gives way. I call that a more inward privation, because it prevented him from recuperating. When a man's heart goes down, it may rise again if his body keeps up; but if his body falls too, the heart will not rise. That is what I understand our Lord to mean when He says, "If the salt has lost its savor, wherewith shall it be salted?" (Matt. 5:13)—if the vital stream itself is low, what can restore joy? Still Job blanches not. No complaint falls from him. His deepest sense is that of acquiescence in the divine will, "The Lord giveth and the Lord taketh away: blessed be the name of the Lord" (Job 1:21).

Then comes the removal of a fourth garment—human

sympathy. Job's friends visit him, and in accordance with the Jewish view of suffering they assume that he must be a special sinner. At first by gesture and then by words, they convey their impression that he has done something to deserve it. And now for the first time his great heart gives way. You have seen a cloud that has hovered overhead all the afternoon touched at last by a freezing vapor and burst forth in torrents. So is it with Job. He has borne up all through the day—borne poverty, bereavement, sickness; but when the freezing vapor touches him, the fountains of the great deep are opened, and the flood descends.

JOB'S DESPAIR AT THE THEORY OF HIS FRIENDS

He has endured calamity; but that his calamity should be made a sign of worthlessness is too much. The explosion is simply terrific; it sweeps all before it. Yet it is not illogical; there is a method in its gusts of passion. Let me try to gather up the threads of argument which the blast carries on its bosom. Let me endeavor to paraphrase the spirit of these remarkable utterances in which Job expresses his indignation at the theory of his friends.

"Tell me not," he cries, "that I have deserved it! Do not say that in any special sense I have incurred the displeasure of the Almighty! I know I have sinned after the manner of Adam's race. How shall a man be just before God? If called to the bar of judgment, could he answer for one of a thousand faults?

"But that is not what you mean. You want me to believe that I have been a special sinner, a sinner above the average. My life refutes the charge. Measured by the common standard, my record is pure. The blessing of him that was ready to perish came upon me, and I caused the heart of the widow to sing for joy. I was eyes to the blind and feet to the lame. When the poor heard, then they blessed me; when the eye saw, then it gave witness. I delivered the fatherless and the widow and him that had no helper. Mine integrity I will hold fast and never let it go; my heart will not reproach me as long as l live.

"But suppose it were otherwise; suppose I were the deep-dyed sinner you picture. Is this pain the way to convict me? If your God wishes me to feel my sin, why does He send me a physical suffering and physical weakness which make it impossible for me to feel anything at all? Why does He seal up my transgressions in a bag—where they cannot be seen? Why does He sew mine iniquities in sackcloth—where they cannot be felt? Why does He break me with a tempest if He wants me to have a vivid consciousness of anything whatever?

"Does the sense of sin come from mutilation, from curtailment, from paralysis of the nerves? Does it not come from expansion, from exaltation, from increasing nearness to God? If I am to abhor myself and repent in dust and ashes, it must be not in the hour of depression but in the hour of revelation—the hour when I meet with God. I cannot accept your explanation of my great and grievous pain."

JOB'S PATIENCE—THE POWER
TO WAIT WITHOUT A REASON

But now in the light of this outcry the question arises, Why do we speak of Job's patience? He has borne bravely three calamities—the three sent from God; why has he sunk before the one sent by man? He has accepted poverty, bereavement, sickness; why has he cried out at the mere suggestion that these are penalties? And why, in spite of that vociferation, has his name been handed down as a synonym for patience? He has stood the hurricane and the tempest, but he has been made to cry out by the lashing of a single wave! Does not the fact of being fretted by so weak a foe deprive him of all right to be the representative of those who wait for God?

I answer, "No"; and I feel sure that the answer will be echoed by the Great Gallery. I am convinced that in the view of the artist the patience of Job is never so conspicuous as in his outcry. Not in spite of but by reason of that outcry has he earned his right to a place among those who wait for God.

Why did Job cry out? Was it not in the interest of patience? Was it not patience that made him cry out? His friends wanted to rob him of his patience—to take away his power to wait without a reason. Is not that just the definition of intellectual patience—the power to trust when there is no light, the ability to possess one's soul in the absence of all explanation of that which afflicts it? Unless we grasp this thought, the personality of Job is meaningless—he is simply an impatient child. But if his impatience springs from the fact that his friends wish to rob him of his patience, if his outcry is caused by his desire to be allowed to wait for God, then, religiously and artistically, the whole portrait is illuminated, and the claim of Job to his traditional virtue receives triumphant vindication.

JOB'S FRIENDS WANT TO
ALTER HIS ATTITUDE OF PATIENCE

Now, the friends of Job are really in this position. They want to alter his attitude of patience. They say: "It is not enough for you to believe that it will be all right some day. You must be able to trace the cause of your calamity. You must be able to put your hand upon some dark deed of your past life, or"—as Elihu puts it— "upon some unspoken principle of evil which has not yet issued in a deed, but which God sees in the silence of your soul."

Put yourself in the place of Job under these circumstances. Imagine that you were passing through a season of bereavement. The light of your eyes has been extinguished, and you are sitting disconsolate in a silent room. Suddenly a solemn bell rings; and draped in black, there enter three figures—Eliphaz, Bildad, and Zophar. They take you by the hand and say, "My friend, God is dealing with you in chastisement. You have been too fond of the world. You have been living for the hour. You have been giving to earthly things the honor which is due to His name. Therefore He has spoken to you in His anger; He has withered your gourd. Humble yourself and confess your sin."

Would you not be disposed to answer, "Am I bound to take such a view? In a world where so much seems arbitrary, where for a time 'the tabernacles of robbers prosper,' where the good are often clothed in sackcloth and the wicked wear the purple robe, am I bound to believe that this is a chastisement to m? Will you not let me keep my patience? Will you not let me trust my God without a theory? Will you not let me believe that in some way unknown to me things are working together for good? Why do you deny me the privilege of the men who wait for God?"

JOB PROTESTS IN FAVOR OF PATIENCE

Even such is the voice of Job. He utters a protest in favor of patience. He appeals from the God of his friends to his own

God. He says, in the spirit of a Greater, "My Father! behold, You come to me in clouds! Life has been overcast for me; the hosannahs are hushed, the palm leaves are withered, the friends of summer days have made their flight in the winter. Men want me to try to understand You, 'Prophesy unto us, O Christ; who is he that smote You?'

"But I will not try to comprehend You. 'The cup which my Father has given me to drink, shall I not drink it?' I accept in the darkness the burden You have laid upon me; I take it unexplained. I come to You in the night—the unvindicated night. I come in the cold that has no explanation, in the snow that is not accounted for. I accept You in Your mean attire, in Your unattractive raiment, in Your repulsive dress. I do not seek to comprehend You; I take You with Your mystery. Though You slay me, yet will I trust in You and believe that I keep Your favor."

A Second Reason Job's Patience Is Vindicated

But there is a second respect in which the patience of Job is vindicated by his outcry. Can there be any patience without a certain amount of inward outcry? If Job has ceased to pray for his friends—in other words, if he has ceased to care what his friends think of him—where is there room for patience? Is it not just this presence of the inner outcry which distinguishes the patience of Christ from what St. John's gospel calls "the peace which the world gives"—Stoicism?

The Stoic says, "If you will only keep down your feelings, if you will only practice the restraining of the bird when it is about to fly, you will come in course of time to have no emotions; you will be able to walk in the funeral cortage fearless, tearless, passionless." Yes, and I would add, "patience-less." For what you have lost in this case is really patience. You have ceased to wait for anything; you have given up the game. You see a man undergoing one of those little operations which flesh is heir to. He never winces. "What admirable nerve!" you say. And yet, in reality, the calmness comes from exactly the opposite cause. The nerve, so far from being admirable, is dead; the man has lost the necessity for patience.

THE OUTCRY AND STRUGGLE OF PATIENCE

There is a question which must often have occurred to an inquiring mind. Why is it that we Christians, to whom the patience of Christ is a watchword and the surrender of His will a glory, are eager to select that part of His life in which the outcry is most loud and the struggle most apparent? Why do we make our pilgrimage in crowds to the Garden of Gethsemane? Why is to us the dearest spot, the most sacrificial spot, precisely that place where He poured forth His soul with strong crying and tears? We could understand why men who admire patience should repair to the scene of the death of Socrates, but it seems a strange thing that they should always take their journey to a place of human outcry like the Garden of Gethsemane!

But the answer, I think, is clear. We go to Gethsemane in the interest of patience. We feel that the outcry is the proof of the sacrifice. Socrates has become deadened in the nerve that gives pain; therefore he has no outcry. But the outcry of Jesus proves that He has not lost His nerve, not lost His youth, not lost His love of human things. It is easy to be crucified by the world if you have ceased to love the world. It is easy to be crucified by your friends if your friends are looked upon by you as simply so many flies to be brushed aside and forgotten.

But the glory of Gethsemane is that life is still beautiful to Jesus—that, with all its sins and sorrows, it still keeps to Him its pristine glow—that the color has not gone out of the flower nor the song of the bird become silent nor the freshness vanished from the breezes. The world is yet worth living in—bright and beautiful with possibilities, fair with promise, radiant with hope. That is what makes it so hard to be crucified by the sons of men; that is what gives value to the sacrifice. We measure the patience by the strength of the cry.

JOB'S SPIRIT UNQUENCHED

Job also had the spirit of youth. However dark his sky, he had not lost his sense of life's possibilities. Deep down in his heart there was the conviction that the world in which he suffered was an unnatural world. He felt that things ought not so to be and that therefore they would not always so be. Clear through the night his voice kept ringing, "I know that my Vindicator lives, and that He shall stand at the last upon the earth; and, though the process of destruction penetrate even beneath the skin, yet in my flesh shall I see God, whom I shall see for myself, and my eyes shall behold and not another" (Job 19:25).

These are the words of hope, not despair. They show that the nerve is not dead, that the love of life is not extinguished, that the spirit of youth remains. If patience implies an outcry, it is because it implies an outlook. It refrains from trying to understand the way, but nonetheless does it believe in the goal. So long as a man keeps his love, he will keep his capacity for pain; but he will also keep his freedom from despair. Where love is, there is no despair. The wind may be raging fierce and cold around us, there may be no star in our night and no present rest in our journey; but if love is not quenched, the ground for hope is still abiding.

The gate of egress may be unseen, the avenue of outlook may be undetected; but already beyond the tombstone there will gleam the Garden, and above the blood-stained heights of Calvary there will glitter the sunlit peaks of Olivet.

A Prayer

Lord, help me to keep my love! Whatever else I lose, may I never lose my love! Though all the lights go out from my life, let not this torch be extinguished. There is a peace which comes by the death of patience—by ceasing any longer to wait or to expect. There is a peace which is not patience, because it looks for nothing, longs for nothing, prays for nothing. There is a peace which is painless because it is numb—a peace free from struggle because it is dead.

I would not have that gift, O my Father! I have passed through the autumn woods and heard no waving of the leaves, not because there was no wind to blow but because there was no sap to nourish. I would not have that gift, O my Father! That is the peace of the grave.

But Your peace is the peace of the ocean. It is the calm that holds depths beneath it. It is not the rest of lifelessness but the rest of balance. Your patience is the patience not of spentness but of expectancy; it rests "in hope."

Bring me Your peace, O God! Bring me the peace of pulsation, the calm of courage, the endurance that springs from energy. Bring me the fortitude of fervor, the repose through inner radiance, the tenacity that is born of trust. Bring me the silence that comes from serenity, the gentleness that is bred of joy, the quiet that has sprung from quickened faith. When I hear You in the whirlwind, there will be a great calm.

For Further Study and Reflection

1. What are four types of despair?
2. How is Job's mission simply "to bear" rather that "to do"?
3. Does the sense of sin come from God's judgment and a sense of depression, or does the sense of personal sin come from nearness to God and the sense of revelation?
4. Why does Job cry out at his friends' condemnations but not at his great earthly losses?
5. Why can we measure the patience by the strength of the outcry?

6

ISHMAEL THE OUTCAST

I n the lands of the Western world there is a type that has always been greatly admired—the unconventional man. The West is the atmosphere of freedom. It is the home of progress, the nursery of the new. To step from the line of routine, to initiate a fresh idea, to be recognized as in some sense out of the common has been in the West a prevalent object of ambition.

But in the lands of the East it has been otherwise. Here, the greatest glory is to be time-worn, antiquated, unrepaired. Enter any national gallery of the old world, you will find many noble qualities represented. But there is one type of man whom you will not find represented—the man who diverges from the traditions of the past. All the figures of these galleries repudiate independence. None wishes to be deemed original; none wants to be thought an innovator on former days.

Confucius tells you he is merely a restorer. Lao-tsze tells you he is following the old "fixed way." Buddha tells you he is but one of many incarnations. China worships her ancestors; India reverences her caste; and with both the reason is the same—the sense that the old is better than the new and that the path of wisdom must ever lie upon the lines traced by our fathers.

But there is one exception to this rule of the ancient world. It occurs in that one gallery which is not national—the portraits of Israel. Here, as elsewhere in the East, there is a reverence for the past; the Garden of Eden lies in the background, and the times of old are the times of glory. But here, unlike those other galleries lit by the rising sun, there is a place prepared for divergent forms. I say "a place prepared." It is not merely that the men outside the caste have their names recorded—India would have done that.

ISRAEL'S TOLERANCE OF PECULIARITY

The peculiarity of the Hebrew Gallery is not that it has recorded the names of its rejected portraits; it lies in the fact that it has admitted portraits which have been rejected elsewhere. It has made room for those diverging forms which the artists of neighboring lands have cast as rubbish to the void. To drop all metaphor, Israel has from the very outset provided a place for the pariah—has opened a door of entrance to the man whom she has herself turned out.

We speak of Israel as a "peculiar" nation. So she is, and the most peculiar thing about her is just her tolerance of peculiarities not her own. We are all to think of this as an exclusive attribute of gospel times. It is not the Gospel; it is its flower, but you will find this tolerance at the root. Christianity was not a revolution; it was a culmination, a climax. It brought to the surface what had long been slumbering underground. It was to Judaism what the autumn is to the spring—a manifestor, a discloser. You will see its germs in Genesis, its examples in Exodus, its precepts in the Prophets. Not without reason in the plan of Providence was the land of Judah chosen as the theater of that Gospel whose province it is to gather the waifs and strays of humanity. No other soil was so prepared for such a seed.

THE HEBREW IDEA OF PATRIARCHAL GOVERNMENT

As the representative of this outlawed class, I have selected a very early portrait—the portrait of Ishmael. He is the Great Gallery's first pariah, its first outcast from society. Cain was not an outcast from society; there was no society in his day; his banishment was from the presence of the Lord. But Ishmael was born in an age of culture, in a scene of culture. He came into the world when the world—the Hebrew world, at least—had begun to be social. Brotherhood was in the air; family life was in the air. A section of mankind had formed the bold and grand design of transforming the idea of empire into the idea of a household.

They had begun to call the king their "father." That is the root idea of patriarchal government—that the names of sovereign and subject should be replaced by the names of father and son. To be banished from such a society was ostracism indeed.

To any man who had breathed the patriarchal atmosphere, the expulsion from that atmosphere was death in the desert. It was to exchange the home for the highway, the brotherhood of man for the breath of misanthropy. No modern condition of exile can represent the exile of a man put out of the patriarchal caste. Modern exile is a change of land, but it need not be a loss of the old country's sympathy. Expulsion from the patriarchal fold was not necessarily a change of land at all; the outcast could live within sight of his former home—is it not written of Ishmael himself, "He shall dwell in the presence of all his brethren" (Gen. 16:12)?

But the sting lay in the fact that the brotherhood itself was broken. The banishment was not one of space; it was one of spirit. It was a separation from sympathy, an isolation from interest. The man might live in the presence of his brethren, but he must live as a stranger to them. He had become a mere individual. He had no family tie, no blood of kinship. He was divided from his comrades of the past by something more impassable than any wall—a thought of the mind.

ISHMAEL'S EXILE

What brought Ishmael into this exile? What has given him the distinction of being in the Great Gallery the first portrait of a pariah? As in nearly all cases of social ostracism, he owes it partly to his misfortune and partly to his fault. For one thing, he had the misfortune—for an Eastern—of being an unconventional man. He is described under the simile of a wild ass. In colloquial English that would be a term of contempt; in literary Hebrew it is a term of admiration. The idea is that of impetuous brilliancy. It depicts a man of noble impulses unable to restrain these impulses, rushing to realize his goal with wonderful, majestic, but unreasoning speed. He has nothing but his individual convictions to support him. The spirit of the age is at variance with his spirit. His views are not the common views. His opinions are deemed eccentric; they place him in an isolated position, in a position of general antagonism, which the narrative indicates by the prophecy.

"His hand shall be against every man and every man's hand against him" (Gen. 16:12). But to that position he adheres. In an age when private judgment brought ostracism and when ostracism meant banishment from all sympathy, he bravely faced the storm. He raised his testimony against the united testimony. He set up the authority of his individual conscience in opposition to the use and custom of the whole community. His figure in the Gallery is the figure of a man in fight with all the world— outnumbered but unsubdued, proscribed but protesting still.

ISHMAEL'S CONVICTION

What was that individual conviction for which Ishmael strove? In the abstract, I think, it was something which was right. He had been born to great possessions—messianic possessions. His mother Hagar was an Egyptian slave who had fled to the tent of Abraham and had become the handmaid to his wife Sarah. Sarah was childless, but she retained unbroken her empire over the heart of Abraham. Abraham was eager to have an heir, but he never dreamed of repudiating his first marriage tie. He had preferred to contract an additional marriage.

At the suggestion of Sarah herself he had espoused the slave Hagar, and the fruit of their union was Ishmael. But here came the sting of the position. Hagar, though a wife, was still a slave. He had not wed her to set her free, but to make her the medium in bringing an heir to Sarah. Ishmael was not to stand for *her* son, but for Sarah's son. Abraham was never more loyal to Sarah than in his union with Hagar. It was for Sarah he formed the union; it was for Sarah he desired posterity.

When Ishmael was born, he was made, officially, the child of Sarah. His real mother was denied all right to her maternity. She was only an instrument for the transmission of the kingdom. She must go back from her marriage to her drudgery, to her slavery. She must resume her menial duties to Sarah. Her seeming elevation to dignity had made it all the more needful that she should be reminded of her continued lowliness. The prospective destiny of her son Ishmael might mislead her, might tend to make her forget that she was still a bondwoman. That fact must be recalled to her remembrance. Ishmael could only be the heir of Sarah on the supposition that Hagar was nobody—a creature without rights, a thing of goods and chattels. By word and deed the fact of her nothingness must daily, hourly, be brought home to the heart of this Egyptian.

ISHMAEL'S PROTEST

In this atmosphere the boy Ishmael grew. He was the heir to a kingdom, and in the court of his future kingdom his mother was a downtrodden domestic slave. Was it conceivable that the heart of the boy should not burn with indignation? Measured by contemporaneous law, there was nothing unjust in the incongruity. But the unconventional man never measures anything by what is contemporaneous; he judges everything by the end of the world and how it will look then. Ishmael saw his actual mother in the position of a menial to his adopted mother. He saw her subjected to daily indignities. He heard in private her vehement complaints. He listened to her assertions of a right to be equal to Sarah, of her claim to be treated as the wife of Abraham.

Is it surprising that in his deepest soul he should have uttered a protest against the spirit of his age? He was a youth of noble impulses; the proof is that he had won the heart of his father Abraham—the most chivalrous of men. Can we wonder that the depths of his nature should have risen up in antagonism to the customs of his land and the usages of his time?

A REAL HEIR IS BORN

By and by something happened—the unexpected happened. A real heir was born to Sarah—the child Isaac appeared. And now Ishmael was supplanted; all his hopes were withered. I do not think these hopes had all been selfish; I doubt not the youth had said to himself "When I become head of the state, I will set my mother free." So far as he was concerned, that prospect was gone now. He should have considered, however, that with the birth of the real heir Sarah had no longer the same motive for keeping Hagar a slave; he should have remembered the native generosity of Abraham. He did not remember it; and this, I think, was the fault added to his misfortune.

Ishmael seems to have thrown off the mask which had hitherto concealed his irritation. His tone became mocking, satirical. What form his satire took, I cannot tell. Perhaps he sneered at the puny, delicate child on whom was to devolve the kingdom—for I have elsewhere expressed the opinion that the Isaac of the Gallery is an invalid. Perhaps he suggested that the birth was an imposture—that the child was not that of Sarah. Whatever he said was said recklessly, publicly. He used no prudence; he made no effort to hide his feelings. He selected the most prominent occasions for his invectives; he spoke where he would be overheard.

I think he spoke with a view to be overheard. I believe he was tired of his equivocal position, of his mother's equivocal position; he felt humiliated by eating as a dependent the bread of which he had been born to be the dispenser. He preferred a life of independent poverty to a life of luxurious vassalage; he panted to be free.

ISHMAEL AND HAGAR ARE SENT AWAY

And he got his desire. The wrath of Sarah was kindled. She had borne acts of disobedience; she had overlooked disregard of her authority, but she could not condone a slight upon her son. She clamored for the dismissal of the Egyptian and her boy; she bore down the unwillingness of her husband. Woman as she was, she was the ruling power in the house of Abraham. Abraham might sway the clan, but Sarah swayed him.

In striking contrast to the other women of the East, this woman rises to our view as the dominant power in church and state—for church and state were then one. She rises to our view as the arbiter of national destinies, as the tribunal from which there can be no appeal. Abraham sinks before her; Mesopotamia sinks before her; her will is law. She waves her hand and says, "Go," and Hagar and Ishmael issue forth from the patriarchal home—to return no more. All that Abraham can do is to make secret provision for their wanderings. Silently he provides the bread and the water and sends out mother and son from the heat of Sarah's wrath into the heat of Beersheba's desert.

When they reach that desert their supply of water is exhausted. Why had Abraham not foreseen this? I think he had foreseen it. If I read rightly the meaning of the Gallery, Abraham knew that in the wilderness of Beersheba there was a well of water that, if once they arrived there, they would find supply without limit. Yet Hagar and Ishmael came and saw not the well. Why? Simply because their nerves were unstrung. When our minds are disturbed, we miss the things that are lying at our feet. In all days, as in the days of the demoniacs in the New Testament, there is a blindness which comes from being possessed by violent passions. It had come to Hagar and Ishmael. Their minds were on fire with anger; their hearts were palpitating with excitement. They were too absorbed within to see anything without.

When the water in the bottle was spent, their strength was spent too; they beheld nothing but the barren sand. The mother bore up better than the son; here again the Gallery shows its respect for patriarchal womanhood. Ishmael was not yet inured to fatigue like Hagar. He had been nurtured daintily, dandled luxuriously; he took badly to the desert; at the prospect of death by thirst, he swooned away.

HAGAR'S PRAYER

But Hagar betook herself to prayer—so I read the narrative. The Egyptian mind was peculiarly religious. It lived more in another world than in this. Its finest architecture was lavished on its tombs; its finest literature is "The Book of the Dead." Hagar partook deeply of the spirit of her land. In her hour of emergency she retired within herself to commune with God. It was not the God of Israel she communed with; it was her own God. But, says the narrative, He answered her.

There is no finer proof of the cosmopolitan spirit of the patriarchal age than that the prayer of an outcast from Israel is answered by the God of Egypt! The answer comes, as all such answers come, in the form of an inward peace—a peace which passed understanding, which defied explanation, but which, just on that account, carried an assurance of succor. For the present, such a peace was all that was required. It sent no supernatural vision, because that was not needed.

The means of refuge lay within the limits of the natural. The well was there, had always been there. What was wanted was a mental calm adequate to the recognition of it. The peace of divine communion brought that. It enabled Hagar to see, to use her faculties of natural observation; as the narrative finely puts it, "God opened her eyes" (Gen. 21:19). When she emerged from her communion, she found the old place changed. The old horror was gone—the horror of prospective thirst. She saw some vegetable product that indicated the presence of water. I do not know that she found water all at once; divine help does not dispense with searching. But the inward peace put her on the right track for searching. It let her see where to go. It led her to fountains of living water and wiped all tears from her eyes—or rather it wiped all tears from her eyes so that she saw the living fountains.

GOD HAS A PLACE FOR THE OUTCAST

But the grand thing—to Hagar, to Ishmael, to ourselves—was the moral bearing of the fact. It had a historical significance. It made the voice of God say, in effect, "Other sheep I have which are not of this fold." It declared that God had a place for the pariah, the outcast—a place for the lands outside the line of Abraham. It proclaimed that the God of Abraham and the God of Isaac was still the God of Egypt and the God of Hagar. It announced that, while He had blessed the seed of the patriarch, He had also a blessing for the nations outside.

The melting of that desert cloud from the eyes of Hagar was a beam of the infinite fatherhood, of the universal brotherhood—a premonition of the truth that God is larger than all our creeds and higher than all our theories. It was Hagar, not Ishmael, that had the vision—and there lies its significance. Ishmael had, after all, the blood of Abraham in his veins; Hagar belonged to a foreign faith and a foreign soil. The God who communed with a woman not included in the orthodox line was already proclaiming to the world that "He is not far from any one of us" (Acts 17:27).

And here the narrative virtually takes leave of Ishmael—merely stating that he rose to be a mighty hunter, that he allied himself with a daughter of Egypt, and that he transmitted an empire to his posterity. He disappears from view as rapidly as one of the steeds of his own Arabian desert. Only once in the record of Genesis do we hear his name again. It is at the end of long years, when the autumn of his life has come. But it is on an occasion so memorable and so significant that it seems a fitting place to say farewell. It is at the funeral of Abraham. There Ishmael and Isaac meet hand to hand in the presence of death. It is a strange meeting.

The pariah and the prince, the man who had lost his kingdom and the man who had supplanted him, the wild undomesticated huntsman and the life immersed in the cares of the home—these at last walk side by side in the fellowship of grief. From the heart of Ishmael all bitterness is gone. In the presence of death he forgets everything but the memories of love. He remembers Abraham as the father who had loved him—who had never ceased to love him; the hour of his expulsion from home is drowned in that bottle of water which was provided for his sustenance. He remembers Isaac as the little delicate child who had come in his way without knowing it and who ought not to have experienced his anger.

Thus death softens all our bitterness. It is one of those touches of universal nature which make the whole world kin. It reveals the common frailty, and there is nothing which unites us like a sense of the common frailty. Ishmael was divided from Isaac by the thought of the mountain; they were joined again by the sight of the valley. They were constrained to walk together by the falling of the evening shadows.

Millenniums have passed since that day, and the old order has given place to the new; yet Ishmael and Isaac are walking together still. The revolving centuries have again brought them to evening time. Islam and Israel are living still. In a new world these old forms remain. The child of the bondwoman and the child who received the inheritance of Abraham are still found walking hand in hand, contemplating that former glory which has been laid in the dust of death.

A PRAYER

I bless You, O Lord, that You have a place for the outcast—for the man who has gone over the line. I thank You that he who comes to You is in no wise cast out, even though he comes by an unusual way. I praise You that You have a revelation for the Hagars of the world—for those whom many have deemed in

Egyptian darkness. Enable me to realize that even in their desert there are springs!

I often speak of the wells of Baca—the wells for Your covenanted people; but I forget the wells of Beersheba which are prepared for the men of the wilderness. I forget that for them also You have revealing messages, openings of the inner eye. Help me to remember it, O Lord!

Help me to remember that my dividing lines are not Your dividing lines. Help me to remember that You have a star which leads to Bethlehem those who have missed the morning sun. Help me to remember that You have songs of Christian glory not included in the choir of the prophets. Help me, above all, to remember that the springs which Your angel discloses are often just in the places which I have pronounced dry parched land.

Increase my hope for man, my sense of man's possibilities. In the hour when I despair of my brother, let me see what You see; let me hear what You hear—the rushing of underground waters, the promise of a life that shall make the desert glad. The desert will to me be already glad when I learn that in Hagar's wilderness there are secret wells seen by You.

For Further Study and Reflection

1. Prior to Isaac's birth, what was Ishmael's position in Abraham's family? What was his mother Hagar's position in the family?

2. What was Sarah's position and influence in Abraham's family?

3. How did Abraham provide for Ishmael and Hagar in the desert?

4. How is the God of Abraham and Isaac also the God of Egypt and Hagar?

5. Where does Ishmael reappear in the story of Abraham?

7

LOT THE LINGERER

The figure of Lot has already met us in traveling through the life of Abraham. But in a book of representative men he cannot be dismissed with an accidental interview. To be seen fairly, a man should be seen by his own light. His portrait should be taken when he is standing alone. A face of average comeliness will look very plain when it is placed beside one of extreme beauty; yet, when seen apart, it may have a charm of its own.

Lot makes an excellent foil to Abraham. Abraham's is a face of extreme beauty, and any ordinary countenance will suffer if placed beside it. But it does not follow that Lot himself might not contrast favorably with many on his own plane. In point of fact he did exhibit a certain beauty of aspect when he was not in the presence of Abraham. When he stands in the midst of Sodom, he looks so remarkably well that his name has been handed down to posterity as one of the world's superior souls; he is called "just Lot."

Let us consider, then, the man in himself. What is his place among representative men? What class does he stand for amid the various orders of humanity? That is the one question, the crucial question. Everything else about him is accidental; but the point of Lot's contact with a common phase of human nature, the sphere in which he meets with an experience repeated in all time—this is the abiding thing; this is the permanent element in the man.

LOT STANDS STILL
There are two words in the Bible narrative which seem to me

to express in one brief sentence the place of Lot amid the phases of humanity—"Lot lingered" (Gen. 19:16). I would say his distinctive position is that of the man who falls behind in the march of civilization. He does not go back; he never could be classed among the lapsed masses. His characteristic is that at a certain point of the road he stands still and allows his comrades to move in advance of him. Lord Macaulay, in one of his *Essays,* raises the problem, Why has the navy of Spain declined? He solves it by the answer that it has not declined but that the increase of other navies has left it in the rear. Whether this is the solution as regards Spain, I cannot tell; but it is the answer which may be given to all who put the same question regarding the tardiness of that ship of life which we call Lot.

Lot is behind the others not because he has lost speed but because the others have gained speed. He stands where he was. In a metaphorical sense he has become what his wife is said to have become in a physical sense—a pillar of salt. He has been crystallized into an inert mass which marks only one stage of a journey.

LOT IS LEFT BEHIND ABRAHAM

This man was, originally, marching abreast with humanity. He had joined the band of Abraham—that first missionary band among the sons of men. He had attached himself to the cause of those whose object was to carry the blessings of culture into lands of darkness and to bear the lamp of knowledge into scenes of ignorance. It was a stream of high civilization which was seeking to irrigate the nations. Nothing could have been more fair than Lot's morning; it promised a fine afternoon. But for him there has come no afternoon; his day is still but beginning. The afternoon has come to others. It has come to Abraham, to Isaac, to Jacob, but not to him; he stands yet where he first stood—on the confines of that missionary march which he had been expected to pursue.

Now, there is nothing unusual in this. It is quite a common thing to see a whole community of men left behind by a stream of civilization; you cannot pass through any city without seeing it; you cannot pass from the city to the country without observing it. In every age of culture there are to be seen those who have lingered behind, who remain yet in the primitive condition of ages long ago. But I wish to direct attention to a new light which the case of Lot throws upon these.

The common saying is that the men left behind are the physically unfit. Those who pursue the march are thought of as the strong, the active, the able-bodied; they who have lingered on the road are taken to have been the weak, the frail, the lives destitute of animal vigor. But in this case of Lot, it is entirely the reverse. Lot is left behind not because he has too little of the physical but because he has too much. He is left behind because his animal nature is stronger than that of his comrades.

Abraham and those who follow him are animated by a sacrificial impulse; they survive by a crucifying of the flesh. Lot is left behind by reason of a fleshly impulse and an inability to resist that impulse. He is not driven to the wall; he believes he is driving others to the wall. He looks upon himself as the really progressive man of the company, the only man who is truly making his way in the world. In his own eyes he is the object of natural selection, the chosen favorite of fortune. It is by and in the exercise of a physical passion that this man is interrupted in the race of life.

LOT'S AVARICE

What was this physical passion? It was avarice. It was the glitter of a great possession that arrested the steps of Lot and chained him to the place forevermore. He saw a fertile field, and he said, "I will make this mine; I will settle down here."

Every race has, in my opinion, a special sin. Rome has her pride; Greece has her voluptuousness; Babylon has her extravagance. I think the special sin of Israel was avarice. I think avarice is the sin attributed to the man in the Garden of Eden— the primeval Adam covets a tree not his own. The trait becomes hereditary; it is repeated all down the stream. We see Cain envying a brother's prosperity. We see Jacob aspiring to another's birthright. We see Esau selling his soul for a mess of pottage. We see Achan hiding a Babylonian garment. We see Gehazi accepting unlawful gold. We see Dives—the parabolic representative of the national sin—allowing a starving beggar nothing but the crumbs from his table.

When Paul says "the love of money is the root of all evil" (1 Tim. 6:10), he has his eye upon his own land. The native of another land might have given another root; the Roman might have stigmatized pride, or the Greek sensuality. But to Paul the Jew, the root of evil was the sin most contagious to the nation—the love of money, the spirit of avarice.

PROSPERITY BRINGS DIVISION

Now, this was the sin which has caused Lot to linger. He has been made stationary by avarice. It is through a grasping spirit that he has been shunted from the line of progress. That grasping spirit was developed not by the experience of want but by the hour of prosperity. As long as the missionary band of Abraham was in struggle, it remained in unity. In the day of storm and stress it revealed no discrepancy. Abraham and Lot walked together with seemingly equal steps as long as it was shadow; it was the dawn that displayed their inequality.

While their life was a common struggle in the wilderness, they had but one interest—the desire to maintain life. But when the storm and stress subsided, when the sun of prosperity began to shine, when the vision of golden fields flashed before the eye with the promise of coming harvests, when the desert broke forth into singing and the wilderness blossomed as the rose, then it was that the difference of the men appeared.

It was in prosperity that the lives parted asunder. It is prosperity that reveals our power of being generous or our want of that power. Poverty makes the open heart and the narrow heart indistinguishable, but the rising sun of fortune shows their contrasted colors. Is it not written of the wheat and the tares, "Let both grow together until the harvest" (Matt. 13:30)—the time of prosperous ingathering. In the time of undergroundness, in the day of struggling growth, wheat and tares are undiscriminated; but when the harvest is come, when the buried life emerges, when the field is waving with yellow corn and plenty crowns the year, then the wheat and the tares are severed, and Lot and Abraham assume their separate spheres.

PROSPERITY, NOT WEAKNESS, INFLUENCES A BACKWARD POSITION

Now, I want just to remark parenthetically that many a lingerer on the road of culture owes his backward position to the flush of

prosperity rather than the blast of adversity. Those who occupy
the rear are indebted for that place more frequently to absorption
in physical pleasure than to the experience of physical weakness.
Some, doubtless, have been crushed out of the way—not, I think,
the majority. The majority have been rather the violent than the
men taken by violence; they are those who have grasped with
too much insistence at a present object and ignored the things of
the future. The main cause of arrest in human development has
been avarice for the object of the hour.

Lot is not an exceptional case; he is a fair specimen of his
class. Arrested development has more root in a deviation from
moral rectitude than either in intellectual stupidity or in physical
incapacity. The larger number of its victims have become its
victims by yielding to the animal impulse which prompts to
seize the present moment in preference to all other moments.
They have been dominated by a malady which is distinctly moral; they have succumbed to avarice, and avarice is a form of sin.

ALL SIN BASED IN AVARICE—
THE DESIRE FOR PERSONAL MONOPOLY

It is my opinion, indeed, that if keenly analyzed, every sin
will be found to be some form of avarice. All self-indulgence,
all debauchery, all licentiousness, all jealousy—even love's jealousy—are but the forms of the one passion—the desire for personal monopoly. If this passion were exercised to the full, I
conceive it would constitute what is called the sin against the
Holy Ghost (Mark 3:29; Luke 12:10).

If the fruit of the Spirit is the love of humanity, the absence of
the Spirit must be the exclusive love of self. Perhaps no human
soul has ever reached that absolute stage of privation. I think we
are saved from committing the sin against the Holy Ghost by the
fact that no man's avarice is complete, that even the most love-
less soul has a little corner in its heart kept vacant and kept
green for somebody.

COVETING MATERIAL POSSESSIONS

But, while all sin is a form of avarice, the name of that vice is
usually limited to a particular phase of the desire for monopoly—
the coveting of material possessions. This is the form which it

has always assumed in the Jewish economy. We have taken Lot as its representative and Lot's lingering as its typical result. And now there arises a question.

Why is it that this man, type as he is of his nation's besetting sin and condemned through that sin to an arrest of development, has yet come down to posterity with the epithet of "just"? He is lauded in spite of his lingering; he is commended notwithstanding his covetousness. Why? Should we not have expected unqualified disgrace? Whence this tone of respect? Whence this ascription of justice to a man of avarice?

I answer, because there is an avarice which is compatible with justice and because Lot belongs to that particular school of avarice. In the sphere of worldly possession I recognize three classes of men—the generous, the avariciously fraudulent, and the avariciously just. The generous man is eager to spend; the avariciously fraudulent man will sink all principle for the sake of gain; the avariciously just man is bent on being rich within the range of principle. To this last order belongs Lot.

You would never class Lot in the list of thieves and robbers. He would die sooner than steal. His is a thoroughly legal mind. His motto is, "Render unto every man his due." Nothing will induce him to fall below the claims of justice. But he would be equally pained to go beyond them. He will give to no one less than his due, but to no one will he give more.

Lot might be described characteristically as the man who never gives a discount. Justice is his watchword, but it is justice pure and simple, never sinking into fraud but never rising into generosity. Twenty shillings in the pound is his ideal—not nineteen, not twenty-one. He will do what is right but not what is kind, not what is overflowing. His verdict is, "To the law and to the testimony"; if he has agreed with you for a penny a day, you will not prevail on him to add a single farthing.

LOT—A JUST MAN MADE GENEROUS

The epistle to the Hebrews says that in the upper sanctuary there is a place set apart for "the spirits of just men made perfect" (12:23) which I understand to mean "the spirits of just men made generous." That is the place in the future heaven which I would appoint for Lot. He was on earth a just man; he never transgressed the principles of justice by deficiency. But he ought to have transgressed them by excess. It was well to give no less than his neighbor's due, but he should have been able to give more.

The perfection of the heavenly state requires that justice should be supplemented by generosity. The state of the avariciously just in the present world is high in comparison with the state of the avariciously fraudulent. Yet I should say that the latter will be more easy to convert than the former. A fraudulent man knows that he is wrong, but it is very difficult to convince a man of bare justice that he is anything less than a saint. Like the Pharisee in the temple, he will give a catalog of all the debts which he has duly paid and will thank God that he is superior to other men.

Victor Hugo in *Les Miserables* has introduced a very striking portrait which gives expression in an exaggerated form to the difficulty here indicated. I allude to the portrait of the constable Jabert. This man has always been scrupulous for observing and enforcing the exact letter of the law. The rigid fulfillment of this undeviating routine has become a conscience with him. One day he is betrayed into an act of leniency towards a prisoner. His remorse for that leniency is so great that he commits suicide. The pain of transgressing the law of justice by performing a generous deed has been too much for him; it has been as great as would have been the pain of transgressing the law of justice by performing a deed of meanness. He has felt himself as much degraded by his act of magnanimity as if he had perpetrated an act of baseness. The incident is only an exaggerated illustration of the self-complacency which belongs to the avariciously just.

The crucial instance of Lot's character is his appropriation of the lion's share in the partition of territory with Abraham. The incident illustrates both his justice and his ungenerosity. He did not take the land by force. He was told by Abraham to make his choice of a locality; he selected the finest spot. Legally, he might easily say, "I have done no wrong." Measured by law, he certainly had not; measured by grace, he had. I would describe his choice of the lion's share as not illegal but ungracious. It was within the rights of law, but it was outside the limits of generosity.

Why had Abraham given Lot a choice at all? Because Lot's

servants had been a torment to Abraham, had created strife and
wrangling within the band. Lot should have remembered this
and should have moderated his desires. He should have remembered also that Abraham's was the mission field and that the
mission field ever deserves the best. Lot was choosing land for
his own benefit; Abraham was choosing land for the benefit of
the kingdom of God. All this made Lot's choice ungraceful,
ungracious.

LOT'S UNGRACIOUSNESS LEADS TO STAGNATION

The selfishness of the choice has brought its own penalty—
stagnation. The failure of Lot did not come from the territory in
which he settled down; it came from the fact that he did settle
down. If Lot had made his possession a mission field, it would
have thriven; but, instead of adapting it to culture, he adapted
himself to its want of culture. Any piece of ground, under these
circumstances, would have become barren ground—Abraham's
would as much as Lot's.

It is the man that makes the place. Personality is a stronger
force than environment; Abraham would have immortalized the
Plain of Sodom; Lot would have left Mount Moriah in its native
obscurity. Lot chose the rich plain for the reason that the ox
chooses the rich pasture, and he has had the ox's reward; he is
browsing there still.

LOT'S CREDIT—HIS HONESTY

And yet I should be sorry to deny this man his due amount of
credit, nay, his due amount of sympathy. Let us remember that
for such a man it was a very arduous thing to be just, and that
therefore it was a very great victory to achieve that goal. For a
generous nature it is easy to avoid falling short of justice; the
temptation is to exceed justice. But for one by nature avaricious,
it is a brave thing to be just. Honesty with such a man would
need to be more than a policy; it would require to be a passion.

The man who is too covetous to be generous and who is yet
too just to be fraudulent must possess the principle of honesty in
an extraordinary degree of development. From this point of view
I would give my sanction to the epithet by which Lot has descended to posterity. Let him take it—he is entitled to it. A more

sounding epithet would have been untrue. We could not describe him as "loving Lot," "tender Lot," "magnanimous Lot"; but "just Lot" is a phrase which truly expresses his character. He has earned the right to it by reason of the very temptation which assailed him.

The truth is, this man occupies morally that very position which he holds socially; he is the man who lingers. Socially, he is neither among the barbarians nor abreast of the highest culture; he is stationary at a particular point. Morally, he is neither a very bad man nor a very good man; he is a correct man. He stands in the golden mean between baseness and generosity— the plain of justice. Behind him is the valley of humiliation; in front of him is the mount of self-forgetfulness; he belongs to neither. He stoops not to the low; he soars not to the high; he keeps the level plain. He is the middle man, the just man. He has paid his way, though he has paid no other's way. His life has been self-contained, but it has been also self-restraining.

If I were asked to place an inscription on the grave of Lot which would be congruous with the facts of his life, I would write the words, "A man worthy of better things." There are some things which are done so well that we are disappointed they are not done better. Many a schoolboy gives us dissatisfaction in the very points where he is strong; we say, "A lad of such parts should take a higher place." Even thus does Lot impress us.

He dwells in Sodom, but he is far above Sodom. In the midst of an environment of iniquity, he never descends. His family descends; his innermost surroundings become unfavorable to purity; but Lot himself stands firm—he bows not to temptation. A man who could thus resist going down might well be expected to go up. A man who could withstand temptation to descend into the pit should have been winged with aspiration to ascend into the heavens. We feel, in looking at him, as we feel in looking at some unfinished building. The foundation is there; the pillars are there; the various stories are there, but the roof is wanting.

The man is far above the ground, but he is not pointing to the sky. He has surmounted the dust, but he has not reached the gold. He has fulfilled the law, but he has not arrived at love. He is so high that he ought to have been higher.

A PRAYER

O Lord whose nature and whose name is Love, let me not pause short of You! Let me not linger on the march of my pilgrimage at any spot less beautiful than Love! Let me not be content to say, "I have kept the law—I have not struck, I have not robbed, I have not slain." Let me not be satisfied to think, "I have been, in all my dealings, just; from what a height do I look down on Sodom!"

Nay, my Father, but let me rather say, "From what a height do You look down on me!" Instead of fixing my eyes on the valley which I have surmounted, let me lift up mine eyes to the hills which I have yet to climb! Teach me that all my safety comes from looking up—not down! Make me humble by the sight of Your hills, O Lord! What time my heart is lifted up with the pride of its vanished yesterday, bring me to the foot of Your Mount of Beatitudes.

Let me see the distance between my soul and Jesus! Give me a glimpse of the Promised Land to cure me of the pride of present possession. Give me a taste of the grapes of Eshcol to disenchant me of the fruits of Sodom. Give me a strain of the songs of Zion to make me weary of my cherished music. Waft me a perfume of the Rose of Sharon to wean me from the flowers which my hands have gathered. Send me a breath of Your mountain air to teach me the narrowness of what I call my freedom. Lend me one throb of Your pulse of love to tell me the poverty of my reign of law. I shall cease to linger on the Plain of Sodom when my eyes have rested on the Heights of Calvary.

For Further Study and Reflection

1. With whom and for what purpose did Lot begin his journey?
2. How do struggle and scarcity promote unity? How does prosperity promote division?
3. How can all sin be seen as a form of avarice?
4. How is Lot just without being either fraudulent or generous?
5. Why is Lot a man worthy of better things?

8

MELCHIZEDEK THE UNCANONICAL

Cuvier says that if you give him a single bone of any animal, he will tell you exactly what was the structure of that animal. I think some such aid as this would often be of immense value to the biographer. There are cases in which the biographer is required to construct an entire life out of nothing more than a fragment. One of these instances occurs on the very threshold of the Bible history.

There appears in the Great Gallery a deeply veiled figure—a face and form delineated in colors so pale that the spectators have failed to take the impression. The portrait seems designed to picture one seen through a mist. Everything about it is obscure, dim, unrevealing. Yet this figure is more thronged than many of those with clearer forms.

Crowds gather round it; hundreds speculate about it. It is the center of wonder, the source of controversy, the ground of enthusiasm. Men of all ages come to it. Abraham stands before it as a reverent spectator. A psalmist of the Exile stands before it in genuine admiration. Above all, one of the latest of the New Testament seers—the writer of the epistle to the Hebrews—has given an exalted interpretation of its character and aim.

This figure, so attractive by its very obscurity, is Melchizedek. I propose to join the crowd of spectators who are standing in front of him. I will disregard speculation; I will keep to the dim record of fact. There is only a fragment to work upon, but that fragment is beyond measure striking. It is more precious than all the gold of Israel for the simple reason that it is quite distinct from the gold of Israel. It is a metal new to the country and rare in any country. It is a fragment wonderfully unconventional—bespeaking an order of things which is foreign to the scene, foreign to the age in which the fragment dwells.

A RARE AND ORIGINAL PICTURE

Melchizedek is one of the most original figures in the Bible. He cannot be accounted for by genealogy. The writer to the Hebrews does not hesitate to say that he is the most unique figure in the Gallery, with the exception of the Son of Man. That is a startling statement; but I think it is borne out by the facts. In the case of Melchizedek the most striking fact is not the character of the man, but the discovery that the Bible has delineated such a man. Nowhere has the Old Testament been more inspired than in giving us this picture. Nowhere has the Jew reached so high in charity; nowhere has he gone down so deep in sympathy; nowhere has he broadened so wide in liberality.

The thing to consider before all others is not the man but his environment. It is the last environment in which we should have expected such a man, the last environment in which we should have expected the Jew to delineate such a man. The force of the figure lies in its background, its mystery, its mean surroundings. Let us look at this.

THE JEW AND THE CANAANITE

If there was one race which the Jew detested, it was the race of Ham; if there was one family of that race which he specially detested, it was the Canaanite. The Canaanite was his earliest enemy; upon the Canaanite fell his earliest curse. He was associated, to the Jewish mind, with all that was bad, all that was profane, all that was worthy to be exterminated. The man of Canaan was to ancient Israel what the man of Galilee was to later Israel—the dweller in a region which sat in darkness and in the shadow of death. It was the most unlikely thing in the world that to the eye of the Jew anything good should come out of Canaan. He was commissioned to expel the Canaanite—to expel him relentlessly, root and branch, with fire and sword. His warrant for this expulsion was his sense of the Canaanite's badness. It was his interest to think badly of this enemy; the thought lent weight to his arm and gave justification to his blows. It was in the nature of things that he should say of Canaan what was afterwards said of Galilee, "Search and see, for out of this race ariseth no prophet" (John 7:52).

And yet, how stands the case? It is from the hated race of Ham, it is from the specially hated race of the Canaanites, that the artist of the Early Gallery has selected one of his brightest models. This Hebrew hand has painted the image of a spotless hero among the natives of this land of sin and death. Melchizedek was a Canaanite. His birthplace was uncanonical. He belonged to that race which was deemed the enemy of the people of God and which the people of God were commanded to cast out. It was here—in this environment of horror and desolation—that according to the ancient narrative there grew the loveliest flower that ever made the desert glad.

THE "KING OF PEACE"

In that little village of Salem which in the far-off days was to become the great city of Jerusalem, there lived and reigned a chief of wonderfully despotic power. I say "wonderfully despotic" for no carnal eye would have seen the source of his despotism. He had no outward weapons, no standing army, no strong fortifications. He had never engaged in war, never raised the standard against a foe—perhaps never had a foe against whom to raise it. His empire had grown noiselessly. So noiselessly had it grown that men called him "The King of Peace." I should think that was the reason why his capital came to be called Salem; it took its character from the character of its king. A man ruling without weapons was in that day a miracle—a far more wonderful spectacle than would have been the sight of the most triumphant warrior. Men could understand how physical force could preserve order; but that order should be preserved without struggle, without uproar, without the visible exercise of authority, this was a unique thing.

Let us proceed further. What gave this man such a marvelous power? What enabled this unarmed mortal to stand in the midst of a rude population and sway them without a blow? It was their sense of his personal sanctity. He was called not only the King of Peace but the King of Righteousness. And it was their sense of his righteousness that made them peaceable to his sway. The only instance I know the least analogous to this picture is the spectacle afforded by medieval Europe of the unarmed Pontiff directing the physical forces of the world. But even this latter portrait has been painted by friendly hands; that of Melchizedek has been drawn by the hand of an enemy.

Who is it that describes the personal sanctity of this Canaanite? It is his deadly foe. How great must have been that sanctity which could elicit so high a testimony from so unlikely a quarter! If this man's purity of life could dominate the hostile house of Abraham, it is little wonder that his name has been preserved as a desert flower.

Melchizedek did dominate the hostile house of Abraham. Read the fourteenth chapter of Genesis. You will see there a remarkable meeting. Abraham and Melchizedek stand face-to-face. Abraham represents the culture that was coming in; Melchizedek represents the culture that was going out. Yet, for the time being, Abraham is the inferior of Melchizedek. Abraham is the man of war; Melchizedek is the man of peace. Abraham represents earth; Melchizedek is the high priest of heaven. Abraham dispenses to Melchizedek a temporal donation; Melchizedek bestows on Abraham a divine blessing. Nay, I am convinced that the blessing which Melchizedek bestowed on Abraham was nothing less than ordination itself. I am convinced that the patriarchal house of Israel received its first priestly impress from the touch and from the blessing of this venerable and venerated scion of a disappearing culture and of a race that was ready to die.

THE SOURCE OF MELCHIZEDEK'S PRIESTHOOD

Where did Melchizedek get that priesthood which he was certainly credited with possessing and which he probably bestowed? That is the next question which solicits our attention. And to this, I think, the narrative itself gives us the answer. I understand that answer to be, "Melchizedek was the earliest man of his class and therefore was not ordained with hands." The first priest of God in the history of the world must have come from a house not made with hands. He must have derived his ordination not from apostolic touch but from popular suffrage.

Imagine that in a somewhat rude and unconventional community there lived a man of singularly pure and upright life—in manners gentle, in piety fervent, in counsel wise, in prayer powerful, in speech eloquent. Imagine that from far and near the peasants gathered on the hills to hear him and listened breathlessly to his thoughts of God. Imagine that he went in and out among the people inquiring as to their welfare and ministering to their need. Imagine that in their sickness he came to pray for them and that by a singular coincidence those for whom he prayed recovered. Would not these men, however far behind in goodness, receive an extraordinary impression of the power of goodness? Would they not also receive an impression of this man's special power and canonize him in their hearts as a medium for their communion with God?

I have taken a case which has come within my own knowledge. But let us suppose that it occurred not in modern times but in an age when ecclesiastical institutions were as yet nonexistent; would not such a man be an ecclesiastic without orders, a churchman without a church, a priest without the laying on of hands? Such the first priest must have been, and the type of the first priest is Melchizedek.

It is in this light that we must understand the remarkable words of the writer to the Hebrews when he speaks of Melchizedek as "without father, without mother, without descent" (7:3). What he means is that his priesthood was without father or mother or descent. What he says is this: "This High Priest of God was uncanonical. He derived his office from no touch of episcopal hand, from no human genealogy. He was the first of his class; he made his class. He has lighted the torch of priesthood for his successors, but God lighted it for him. The generations that followed him can claim him as their ecclesiastical father, but he himself had no ecclesiastical father; he got his life from God.

"His priesthood came from within. It was his sanctity that made him reverenced. Abraham received his blessing from him, his ordination from him, not because he was the scion of a long sacred line but because he was the personification of righteousness, the emblem of peace. The tribute paid to him was the tribute paid to holiness. He derived his sacred character from no carnal authority but from 'the power of an endless life'—a life without beginning of days or close of years—the Life of the Eternal."

PRIESTHOOD ARISES IN THE HEART

I have sought thus to paraphrase the striking passage in Hebrews. The thought clearly seems to be that the chain of canonicity has its origin in the uncanonical—in the spontaneous and unruled dictates of the individual heart. The writer declares that the beginning of every ecclesiastical chain is something not ecclesiastical but something human. He tells us that the churches of the old world each began in a human soul—in the heart of a single, solitary man. Within this holy temple all other temples had their foundation; within this sacred shrine all other shrines were lighted. In Melchizedek, within the precincts of one heart, was laid the nucleus of all that sanctity which attached to the patriarchal line. The priesthood of a Jacob, the priesthood of an Isaac, the priesthood of an Abraham were all derived; but the priesthood of Melchizedek was all his own—it came from the purity of his inmost soul.

There are, I think, three orders of priesthood in the Bible—the Patriarchal, the Jewish, and the Christian; and at the beginning of each dispensation there stands an individual life whose ordination is not made with hands. The origin of the patriarchal dispensation is the holiness of one man—the man Melchizedek. The origin of the Jewish dispensation is the holiness of one man, the man who got his fire direct from the burning bush—the man Moses. The origin of the Christian dispensation is, from the human side, the holiness of one Man—the Man Christ Jesus.

I should not have dared to make this last comparison if the writer to the Hebrews had not made it before me. But he has. He says that Christ was made a priest "after the manner of Melchizedek" (7:17, 21). I prefer the translation "after the manner" to "after the order." The very peculiarity of Melchizedek is that he belongs to no order. He did not derive his priesthood from that hereditary descent which in patriarchal times was its common source; he was, in this respect, "without father or mother." He was the earliest of his kind.

Aaron got his priesthood from the consecrated hand of Moses; Melchizedek got his from no hand. The difference between Aaron and Melchizedek lay precisely in this, that Aaron belonged to an order, Melchizedek did not.

MELCHIZEDEK AND CHRIST

The point of comparison, therefore, between Melchizedek and Christ is just the uncanonical manner of their ordination. Looking at the matter from the human side and abstracting the attention from theological prejudices, there is nothing to my mind more remarkable than the uncanonical aspect of the Son of Man. He has founded a Church—the greatest priesthood this world has ever seen. He has built a visible house of God—a structure which has filled the largest space in modern history and occupied the center of modern civilization. Yet He Himself stands not in a house made with hands.

The ordination He has given is an ordination which personally He does not possess. The ecclesiastical function has been made canonical by Him, but He Himself has no canonical orders. He has given what He did not get, imparted what He did not receive. We have obtained the flower from His hand, but we have never seen Him pluck it from any garden. He has not been presented with the rose; He has created it; He has obtained it "after the manner of Melchizedek."

I am deeply impressed with the prominence which the Evangelists have given to this feature of the Son of Man—His want of canonicity. It is to my mind the thing which of all others they are most eager to suggest. As a rule, they are chiefly anxious to tell their story; but if there is anything they desire to tell besides their story, it is of the absence of canonicity in the priesthood of Jesus.

JESUS IS LIFE ITSELF

We see the child in the temple performing an act of self-consecration to the service of His Father. We see the youth on the banks of Jordan recognized as independent of the baptism He received. We see the man on the path of beneficence pointing the laboring and the heavy-laden not to the consolation of the Scriptures, not to the counsel of the Hierarchy, not to the cleansing power of the Jewish sacrifices but to His own underived strength: "Come unto Me."

We see the life as it nears its close repair to no human helps or fountains of earthly preparation but illumine itself with a glory all its own: "as He prayed, the fashion of His countenance was altered, and His face did shine" (Luke 9:29). He gave the impression of one having life in Himself—life not derived from other lives. He gave the impression of one who was lighting the world—not of one whom the world was lighting. He gave the impression of one who was creating a fountain—not of a thirsty traveler who had been refreshed by a stream.

He was not made sacred by the touch of sacred things; He touched common things, and they became sacred. He glorified objects which were canonically ignoble; He made suffering holy; He made patience heroic; He made the cross divine. Unconsecrated, He became the source of consecration; He was a priest "after the manner of Melchizedek."

MELCHIZEDEK'S PORTRAIT IS REFLECTED IN THE LIFE OF CHRIST

I have dwelt upon this gospel picture because it illustrates the Old Testament picture—is meant to illustrate that picture. In the absence of any direct biography of Melchizedek, the best description we can give of his priesthood is to say, "It was like the ministry of Jesus." That is what the writer to the Hebrews says, and it conveys a whole volume.

What, now, is the effect of this portrait of Melchizedek as reflected in the life of Christ? What is its historical significance, its abiding lesson? Is it not simply this, that in the last result the most important of all factors is the individual man? Catholic and Protestant alike, if they go back far enough, will arrive at a time when a man's church is in his own house and in his own soul. They will come to a time when a man's glory shines not from without but from within. St. John in Patmos beheld a city of the future in which there was no temple. But if religion is to culminate in the absence of a temple, its culmination will be only like its beginning.

The first man in the Garden of the Lord is ever a Melchizedek. Like the primeval Adam, he stands alone. He is without father or mother or descent. He has received no ordination from the past; he has to make his own paradise. There are no stones in his wilderness which he can make bread. He is the heir to no sacraments, the inheritor of no promises. The desert cannot make him glad; he has to gladden the desert. He is the first rose of summer; and therefore, as truly as the last rose, he is alone. The last rose has lost her companions, but the first has never had companions, and that is equal loneliness. The solitude of Melchizedek is the solitude of the

Son of Man—the solitude of one who is born before his time and who has seen a vision his generation cannot see. Melchizedek burst into flower when the Canaanite was still in the land.

A PRAYER

I thank You, O Father, that You have ever planted Your first rose before the Canaanite has been expelled. I thank You that You have sown the wheat before You have plucked up the tares. I thank You that You have sent Your primrose into my early year.

There are Melchizedeks in the heart while the heart is still only a "land of the Canaanites." My aspirations come sooner than my deeds. Long before I am good I have longings after goodness. You accept me for these longings, O my God! You wait not for the full corn; You tarry not for the autumn ripeness.

You come to the one opening bud in my heart—the one Melchizedek in my Canaan. You come to my first rose—my primrose. You call my life a garden while it is yet a wilderness; I am justified by faith—by mere aspiration, before I have done a single good work. The Canaanites are all within me still; the old habits are there; the old temptations are there. But there is a single Melchizedek among them—the wish of my heart for better things.

You have accepted that solitary flower and called it righteousness. You have beheld my one star and called it Bethlehem. You have seen my one thread of gold and called it Christ. You have heard the faint beating of my heart and called it Calvary. You have received Melchizedek in spite of his environment; in the dark and in the cold You have received him; in the midst of the Canaanites You have received him. Bless the Lord, O my soul!

For Further Study and Reflection

1. Where did Melchizedek come from?
2. How did the Jews view the Canaanites?
3. How did Melchizedek attain his power?
4. Where did Melchizedek's priesthood come from?
5. How is the solitude of Melchizedek like the solitude of Christ?

9

BALAAM THE INCONSISTENT

There are few figures in the Gallery which make one feel so near to modern times as the portrait of Balaam. It is placed in a foreign environment, in a culture long outgrown, in a scene remote from Western experience. It professes to delineate the days of Israel's desert—that period which, of all others, carries us furthest away from present civilization.

Yet, in defiance of these surroundings, the picture speaks to us as a modern man. The desert becomes a city; the plains of Mesopotamia assume the aspect of the streets of London; the distance of the years is annulled, and we stand in the presence of our contemporaries. In a thousand of these contemporaries we meet the form of Balaam. There he stands—undimmed by the mists of antiquity, uncrushed by the crumbling of empires and the dethroning of dynasties!

Three thousand years at least have swept over Balaam in vain. Myriad changes of vesture have signalized the human drama since he stood on the arena of the wilderness; but this man has assumed each new costume, has donned each fresh fashion, has worn each mantle of every age. He remains still his inner self, his original self—one of those forms which make us realize that there is an element in humanity which is the same in all centuries and identical in all climes.

A MAN OF TWO WORLDS

I have taken Balaam as the type of the inconsistent man. He belongs to that widest of all classes—the men of two worlds. The two worlds, however, are heaven and earth—not heaven and hell. He wavers between two principles, but the principles between which he wavers are not good and evil. It would be more correct to say that he is a man struggling between the old and the new.

We have, in my opinion, a wrong view of the character of Balaam. We think of him as a backslider from the faith of Moses, as a man tempted by worldly ambition to desert the God of Israel. A more unjust view cannot be conceived. A man standing on a doorstep may be either coming into the house or going out. Whether he is coming in or going out must be determined by his previous footsteps. Balaam is unquestionably on the doorstep; but he is the man coming in—entering the precincts of the God of Israel. His temptation is not the temptation to retreat; it is the temptation to advance—to become a better man.

The interruption he experiences, the struggle he experiences, is caused by the breaking of light upon darkness—not by the impinging of darkness upon light. Unless we appreciate this fact, we cannot do justice to the character of Balaam. Inconsistent he certainly is, but it is the inconsistency not of one who descends to the moral plain after summering on the top of the mountain but of one who, after long dwelling on the plain, begins in later years to climb the mountain. That he ever reached the summit I do not know; I think the narrative leaves him climbing. But he is climbing—not groveling; and it is in this light we must view him if we would see the full proportions of the man.

THE STORY RETOLD

I think I shall be most true to the delineation of Balaam in the Great Gallery if I place the man in an environment which will be at once equivalent and modern—in other words, if I give the story a parabolic dress. I will try to put ideas in the place of names. If we practiced such a system more, I think we should find that history repeats itself and that the life which we relegate to ancient times is very much the life in which at present we live and move. It is the scenery that makes the difference; the actors are always the same. I will clothe in a modern garb the story of this ancient man.

Once in the olden time, there dwelt in Pethor, a town of Mesopotamia on the banks of the Euphrates, a very distinguished religious preacher named Balaam. He was possessed of extraordinary gifts—splendid imagination, graphic descriptive power, and a wonderful faculty of dramatic representation. These qualities had been fostered by the religion of the country to which he ministered—the land of Moab.

THE RELIGION OF MOAB

The religion of Moab was the worship of a God of nature. By whatever name or names He was called, this was His characteristic in the eyes of that people. The Moabite worshiped the physically beautiful. He adored the objects of the eye. He luxuriated in all beauty that was sensuous. He invested female loveliness with a sacramental value—to the point of exposing religion to licentious temptations. He delighted, above all things, in the vision of mountains. It seemed to him that God's metropolis was there. Wherever he saw physical height, he uncovered his head in adoration. His worship was essentially an aesthetic culture, an admiration of nature's symmetry.

In this atmosphere, as I take it, Balaam had been nursed; from this atmosphere he had received his first breath of inspiration—his poetry. It was at the shrine of Moab his imagination had been lighted. Here had been kindled his sense of the physically sublime. Here had been stimulated his architectural power of constructing lofty imagery. Here had been evoked his facility for graphic description and his faculty for artistic delineation. In all these respects Balaam was the child of Moab.

But latterly there had come into his life a second influence. I say "a second" rather than "another." It did not expel the first but was added to it as a fresh impulse.

THE RELIGION OF THE HEBREWS

There had come to the ears of Balaam tidings of a strange people who had emerged from Egypt into the wilderness and were growing in power and greatness day-by-day. He had heard of their conception of God, and it was to him a novel conception. It was that of a God whose main feature was not beauty, not symmetry, not outward splendor but righteousness. It was the idea of a Being who desired that they who worshiped Him should worship love, truth, holiness—that His votaries should be composed of the men who served their brother man, who sustained the sanctity of home, who were upright in business, stainless in morals, reliable in testimony.

The very novelty took hold of Balaam—the admiration of the internal was such a new thing! He was influenced by the Hebrew movement, but he hid the fact in his heart. He knew that in high places this revival of the religious life was not popular. Its origin was democratic. It was the product of revolution, of rebellion against the authority of Egypt. Kings looked with jealousy upon it; those who favored it were likely to get no promotion. Balaam had been born and bred a conservative. His interests lay not with the masses but with the classes. His influence as a preacher would be shaken if he allied himself with what was deemed not respectable. Prudence counseled him to keep quiet; yet, in the secret hours he often asked himself if this new movement did not supply the missing link in the religious life.

KING BALAK'S OFFER TO BALAAM

By and by there came to Balaam one of those moments of crisis which reveal a man to himself, which force him to examine himself. The office of court-preacher in the royal house of Moab became vacant. King Balak looked round to see if there was anywhere a man of pulpit gifts capable of supporting the dignity of the state religion. His eye lighted on Balaam. He sent a deputation to confer with him. They came to the preacher of Pethor and offered him the tempting charge. They said, "The king wants a man of culture, of imagination, of brilliant secular gifts. He wants a man whose preaching will attract so as to be a counterpoise. He wants him to strike a keynote which shall be a trump of war against that gloomy view of God which is being propagated by these desert revivalists. Will you come, and blow that trumpet?"

Then Balaam began to question himself more seriously. Was he in a position to accept such an office? Had he a right to denounce the revivalists of the desert? Was not their God in a sense already his God? Had He not gained possession of a greater part of his mind than he cared to acknowledge? Was there not something within him which told him that he owed allegiance to more than beauty, more than symmetry, more than the laws of art—that there was a law more potent than any natural force, more binding than any aesthetic sympathy?

And so Balaam declined the call. The call was accompanied by conditions which jarred upon him, which rose against one side of his nature. With a noble self-denial he put the temptation aside; he said, "I will not go."

THE REPEATED OFFER

Then the offer was repeated—in a grander form, with more imposing advantages. A larger deputation came, composed of men of higher position; and with increased pertinacity and enlarged promises the call was pressed on Balaam. The salary was doubled; the privileges were multiplied; the attendant honors were augmented tenfold. Balaam was shaken; he was dazzled by the prospect.

It is here more than anywhere else that the inconsistency of his character appears. If a man refuses on the ground of conscience a post worth a thousand a year, he is not justified in reconsidering the matter if the same post is offered at ten thousand. With Balaam it ought not to have been a money question at all; his conscience should have been equally imperative over a mite as over a million.

But then, the man had two natures; conscience had not conquered all the land. On one side of his being he was still a child of Moab—a lover of the physical. The result was that Moab and Israel began to strive within him—the flesh against the spirit, the spirit against the flesh. The outer man cried, "Take the gold; make yourself comfortable, fashionable, famous!" The inner said, "Do not; do not trick your conscience; let no honors tempt you from the path of honesty."

Balaam, then, like Paul in different circumstances, was caught between these two. He had a desire to depart and be with the king of Moab, but duty bade him remain. He could not decide at the moment; he required time to think it over. He asked the deputation to stay at his house overnight. They consented.

What follows has perplexed all the critics—the "lower" as much as the "higher." Hundreds of devout Christians have sought a solution which would free them from a literal interpretation. As this is a matter not for learning but for imagination, I venture to lift my voice with those of the "chiefest apostles" and to offer with all diffidence a humble contribution to the efforts that have been made to clear the mystery.

BALAAM'S QUANDARY

Balaam went to bed with a tumult in his brain. To go or not to go—that was the question. He laid down his head upon the pillow listening to a dialogue within his own soul—an argument fiercely contested and vehemently maintained. At last nature became exhausted, and he fell asleep, but his waking problem became the problem of his dreams.

In Numbers 22:20 we read, "God came to Balaam at night." I understand the words "at night" to mean "in a dream"; and I think that all the sequel of the chapter, up to verse 35, is a description of this dream.

Balaam thought that the God of Israel stood before him and said, "If the men come to call thee, rise up and go with them." Then he thought that the morning had come and that, in company with the august deputation, he was already on his way. And as he traveled in his dream with a heart still full of misgiving, it seemed to him that he was everywhere beset with barriers.

Suddenly, the ass on which he rode shied and halted. Balaam lashed her, spurred her, goaded her; but it was all in vain. Neither the menace of the voice nor the stimulus of the whip were of any avail. Ultimately, she fell on the ground and began to utter words of expostulation. There are no wonders in dreamland. Balaam is not surprised at the conversational powers of the naturally dumb animal. He seems more impressed with her argument than with her articulation.

THE ANGEL'S MESSAGE

He grows calmer and begins to look around; and then, all at once, the obstacle is revealed to him. There, right in the center of his path, stands a figure with a drawn sword whom he identifies as God's angel and before whom he prostrates himself. The angel warns him that his course is a dangerous one. Balaam offers to return. The angel suggests a compromise. Balaam is to go, but he is to go without any promise on his part. He is to accept the vacant living on the condition that he will only censure the people of Israel when his conscience points to any particular act in which they deserve censure—so I understand the nature of the compact.

BALAAM'S COMPROMISE

With the angel's disappearance Balaam awoke and found that the real morning was come. The various voices of the night had been the various voices of his own mind. But of these, the voice of the angel remained paramount. It seemed to offer a prospect of making the best of both worlds. Was it not likely that, after all, occasions would arise in which Balaam might at once be true to his conscience and acceptable to Moab? Was it not almost certain that the children of Israel would sometimes make a slip that called for denunciation? Was it not absolutely certain that at least isolated individuals of the band would be guilty of trespasses and misdemeanors which would enable him to point a moral that would be dear to the heart of Balak? Had he not found at last a way by which he could both keep his conscience clear and raise his fortunes high? He resolved that he would go.

Now, it will be acknowledged that this compromise put Balaam morally in a very dangerous position. It was practically the position of a preacher whose parish success was proportionate to the amount of sin in the district. The ordinary case of the religious minister is just the reverse; he is deemed successful in proportion as he can give a good report. But when a minister is told that his income will rise with the increase of sin in his parish, he is brought perilously near to a great temptation—the temptation of desiring that sin may abound.

Balaam was placed in circumstances where his material interests came into conflict with his spiritual interests. His material interest was Israel's sin; his spiritual interest was Israel's holiness. He was the auditor of two simultaneous and opposing voices; the one called on him to contemplate the sea's buried dead; the other bade him count its treasured pearls. Which of these voices was to win?

BALAAM'S PREMEDITATION

I think I must answer that the victory remained with the last. I know this is not the common view. We have come to think of Balaam as a man who came to curse the people of God but who, by an involuntary process, was made to utter words of blessing. I submit that such is not the view suggested by the narrative. Let anyone read the twenty-third and twenty-fourth chapters of Numbers and say if he thinks these magnificent words were intended to describe the absence of premeditation. But, indeed, there is no room for argument on this point.

The narrative tells us in express terms that there was premeditation—that the addresses of the preacher were not even impromptu, much less involuntary. It tells us that before delivering his sermons he had moments of communion with God. What he said in public was the result of what he thought in private. Many a cleric has entered his study with a determination to please Moab and has emerged from it with a resolve to bless Israel.

I have known more than one man who has sat down to write a life of Christ from an exclusively human standpoint. In each case he has said to himself, "I must be abreast of the time; I must explain everything by the causes known to Moab; I must avoid all reference to the supernatural—otherwise I shall be deemed behind the age." But as he proceeds in his task, he has found that the Christ he proposes to construct would be more supernatural than the One he seeks to avoid. He has found that to attribute the Christ of the Gospels to natural causes would be to proclaim a real violation of law, a miracle compared to which the healing of the demoniacs would be pure science; and he has been compelled, in the very defense of his scientific reputation, to assume the presence of an influence not measurable by Moabitic lines.

BALAAM MUST SPEAK GOD'S WORD ACCURATELY

Now, this is a parabolic description of the case of Balaam. We may call him an inconsistent man, but his inconsistency appears not in the pulpit but in the study. He enters the study with a naturalistic bias. He is dazzled by the court of Balak, impressed with the honor of being selected as the representative of the age. He would like, if possible, to keep up that reputation—to interpret all texts on the lines of the school of Moab. But as he reads, he is in communion with a larger influence; and ever more and more that influence becomes the dominant one.

He looks at the field of thought from various standpoints, surveys it from different altitudes. But from whatever height he beholds it, he is borne back to the same conclusion—that the fruits of this field have been matured by no earthly sun. Ever as he gazes, the star of Jacob grows clearer and clearer. Ever as he ponders, the destiny of this tribe of the desert shines forth with greater splendor. Ever as he meditates, the origin of this people seems more unique, more inexplicable, more separate from the world's origins. When Balaam comes out of his study, so far as intellectual conviction is concerned, he has made up his mind— has decided for the kingdom of God.

Yet Balaam did not outwardly join the kingdom of God. He refused to denounce it, but he would not become a member. Balak heaped him with contempt and dismissed him, yet he left not the church of his fathers. There must have been something stubbornly loyal about the man to stick to the old ship when he knew it was doomed and when its crew had treated him with scorn!

BALAAM'S ADVICE TO KING BALAK

Balaam parted from the king, but he never abandoned his allegiance. Before parting he gave his sovereign a word of counsel which has handed down his name to infamy but which, I think, has been misinterpreted in its motive. What I understand him to have said is this: "These men of Israel can never be hurt by the word of others; if they are ever to be injured, it must be by their own hand. I propose, O king, a better test of their power than you have offered. You want to see if they can stand your blows; I would ask you to see if they can stand your blandishments. You seek to kill them by floods; can you kill them by flowers? Try them with your temptations; ply them with the allurements, with the seductions, of your city life! If they can resist these, they have proved their right to a unique place in history; if they succumb, they will suffer greater loss than the denunciations of any prophet could ever bring."

BALAAM SPOKE IN GOOD FAITH

This advice, as I have said, has tarnished the name of Balaam with historical infamy. Yet, I think, unjustly. I believe he spoke in good faith and with no malign intent towards Israel. The test he proposed was a sound one. It is the counterpart of that which in the great drama the Almighty accepts for Job. In Job's case the problem was, can man resist the temptations of suffering? In Israel's case the problem was, can man resist the temptations of pleasure? I cannot see that the latter is a whit less legitimate than the former.

I think Balaam both believed and hoped that Israel would stand the test, would emerge from the trial victorious. What motive had he for wishing the contrary? He had no longer any official connection with Balak; he had been dismissed from his service. Did not all his interest lie in the hope that his refusal to curse the children of Israel would be vindicated by the stream of events and that the far-off glory which he predicted for their race would be already prefigured in the eyes of the king of Moab?

The rest of the narrative I can only piece together by the threads of imagination. But it seems to me that the order of events was this: Balaam went back to his home. Moab continued her aggressive policy towards the people of God and formed a league with Midian to bar their way. Israel had no recourse but war. She was bound for the land of Canaan, and her way to Canaan was blocked. If the barrier could not be removed by favor, it must be shattered by force.

Israel advanced to battle. She was small among the nations, but her strength lay in her religious faith. Midian too desired such a strength. On her was to fall the brunt of the battle, and she wanted spiritual support. She thought of Balaam. If that great preacher would stand in her ranks to stimulate the living and to comfort the dying, she believed she would prevail.

BALAAM JOINS MIDIAN AS A PRIEST

Balaam is summoned from his retreat. He obeys. He joins the ranks that are fighting in the cause of his former master, Balak. Not as a soldier does he join but as a priest, as a consoler. In doing so he displayed no inconsistency with his latest conviction; who needs religious consolation so much as those in the wrong?

Balaam fell on the field of battle—in the capacity, as I think, not of a warrior but of a priest. He died helping the enemies of Israel—but the help he gave was such as a man may give to those with whom he agrees not. In his last act he has been numbered among the transgressors by the reckoning of history; he is not included in the visible communion of the people of God.

Yet Balaam remains on the roll of inspired men, yea, of God's inspired men. His words are authoritative. His sayings are pro-verbial; they have become part of Holy Writ; they are quoted; they are sung. Israel is as proud of them as of the utterances of Isaiah. There is no stronger testimony to the truth that the ways of heaven are wider than the paths of earth and that the inspiration of God is larger than the creeds of man.

A PRAYER

O Lord, You have never left Yourself without a witness in any land. Let me not narrow the range of Your Spirit! Let me not say that Your voice can only reach the members of the visible church. Teach me that You have psalmists even in Moab, seers even in Midian.

Often have I marveled at the Balaams of this world. I have seen gifted souls, inspired souls, who have not been numbered with Your congregation; I have heard strains of divine melody which have not come from Your sanctuary; I have read thoughts of sublime beauty which have not issued from Your tabernacle; I have found deeds of sacrificial love which have not radiated from Your visible altar—and I have wondered. Let me wonder no more!

You are larger than Your tabernacle; You are wider than Your altar. You travel on the wings of the morning. In the uttermost parts of the sea I find You. If I say of any spot, "Surely here the darkness will cover me!" I mee You behind the curtain! We do not shut You out by shutting the gates on You; You can enter through closed doors. Your rays are X rays; they pass through my fleshly barriers; they detect my secret wounds.

Do not let me call my brother an infidel because he joins not Your outward church; Your church can join him! You hast recognized hundreds on the road to Emmaus who have not recognized You. You have seen Nathanaels under the fig tree who never knew You were passing by. Increase my charity, O God!

For Further Study and Reflection

1. What two worlds are important to Balaam?
2. How did the religion of the Israelites differ from the religion of the Moabites?
3. On what grounds could Balaam freely curse Israel?
4. How were Balaam's material interests and his spiritual interests in conflict?
5. Did Balaam speak the truth? Were his oracles received from God?

10

AARON THE VACILLATING

There is one type of man who has not always received the sympathy he deserves—the man who has narrowly missed the goal. Of course, those who have narrowly missed and those who have missed by a million miles are historically in the same position; they are all included under the general name—failures. Yet, while historically it may be true that "a miss is as good as a mile," it is, morally, not true. The man who has lost the goal by a final slip of the foot is in a vastly different position from the man who has never come within sight of it.

I am inclined to divide humanity into three classes—the man of success, the man of failure, and the man of shortcoming. I would place the last between the other two. He encompasses by far the largest class among the runners of the race of life. Perfect success is not reached by many; absolute failure is the lot of few; but the narrow missing of the mark is the fate of the large majority of men. Take a survey of those around you. What is their mental average? It is not greatness, it is not smallness, it is not even middle-sizedness; it is shortcoming. It is the missing of the mark by a hairbreadth. It is the absence of one little piece of the puzzle preventing the structure from being pieced together. Our common impression of the men and women around us is not that the chain is brass, but that a link of the gold is missing.

Now, I am very glad that this wide class has not been left without a representative in the Great Gallery. The man chosen as its representative is Aaron. If I were asked to define his place in the

102

Gallery, I should say he is the man who narrowly missed the mark, who came in second. I do not know any portrait of the group that is so suggestive of this quality. It is not, for example, suggested by the portraits of Cain and Esau. These are the delineations of men who were not in the race, whose significance lay in the fact that they were impediments to the running. But Aaron was a real competitor. He was a man who appeared to be the leader of his time. He did not stand to his brother Moses in the same relation that Cain held to Abel, or Esau to Jacob. He had a common cause with Moses. He burned as eagerly for the emancipation of his people; originally, he seems to have burned more eagerly.

AARON AND MOSES COMPARED

If any spectator had looked upon the two brothers before the day of the emancipation and considered their comparative prom- ise of success, he would, I think, have given the preference to Aaron. Aaron was the elder. That itself was little for it had become a proverbial saying that in the Hebrew race the elder should serve the younger. But in this case there seemed to lie with Aaron the maturity of mind as well as years. As the broth- ers stand before us, we are struck with the contrast between them, and it is Aaron who seems to have the higher ground. Moses is shy; Aaron is bold. Moses is reticent; Aaron is outspo- ken. Moses speaks haltingly; Aaron is a man of eloquence. Moses is meek and prone to wait the tide of events; Aaron is an impetu- ous spirit and tends to rush into action. Moses meditates forty years in the desert of Midian; Aaron in that same desert seems to have been doing powerful service in winning the favor of the neighboring chiefs.

And yet the fact remains that Moses was the chosen man, the man selected to be the leader of the rising age. Why is this? The common answer is that he was by nature the weaker vessel, and God selects the weaker vessel. But where do we find that doc- trine—that the principle of divine selection is the natural weak- ness of the object? In 1 Corinthians 1:27 St. Paul writes, "God has chosen the weak things of the world to confound the things which are mighty." Yes, "the weak things of the world"—the things which the world deems weak. That is a very different statement from "the things which God deems weak."

THE PRINCIPLE OF DIVINE SELECTION

The truth is, the principle of divine selection is, and has always been, identical with the principle of natural selection—the survival of the fittest. The men who are chosen by the Great Gallery to carry on the kingdom of God are chosen on distinctly Darwinian grounds—not because they are weak but because they are strong. If Abel is preferred to Cain, it is because he is a fitter man than Cain; if Jacob is preferred to Esau, it is because he is a stronger personality than Esau. Weakness can never be the ground of a selection, either divine or human.

There is a paradox in the choice of the Bible, but it does not lie where it is supposed to lie. It lies in the fact that the Bible has a different estimate of strength from that made by the secular eye. The secular eye sees the things on the surface; it measures the power of work by the power of manifestation. But the Bible looks below. It considers not the power of manifestation but the power of restraint. It judges a man more by his stillness than by his outcry, more by his words unsaid than by his words spoken. To the eye of the Bible it is a ruler's self-repression that makes him great, that proves him strong. The thing it considers essential is not fighting power but waiting power. It deems most valuable what the world calls weak. The qualities it appreciates are just the unbrilliant qualities—the attributes held to be not heroic. It prefers patience to petulance, temperance to temper, vigilance to violence, latent discretion to loud display. All this is expressed in Zechariah 4:6, "Not by might nor by power but by my Spirit, saith the Lord."

BIBLICAL STRENGTH IS TENACITY OF WILL

We may conclude, then, that Moses was selected for a higher post than Aaron not because he was a weaker vessel but because he was a stronger one. Where lay the difference in their strength? It lay within—in the innermost region of all—in the power of will. The Bible's test of strength is tenacity of will. To be immovable like the great mountains, to be steadfast as the solid rocks, is ever its deepest aspiration. The things of nature which it admires are the things which it can think of as tenacious. The tree whose leaf "shall not wither," the city which "shall never be moved," the sun that "shall no more go down," the well of water "springing up eternally," the rainbow which shall be a sign "while the earth remaineth"—these are among its fondest fancies. And all these are to the Bible but the symbols of a deeper tenacity still—the endurance of a human heart, the steadfastness of a human purpose.

AARON LACKED TENACITY OF PURPOSE

Now, the crucial point of difference between Moses and Aaron was this tenacity of purpose. All other contrasts, from the Gallery's point of view, are irrelevant. Aaron had every quality fitted for a great leader but one—tenacity of purpose. He was eloquent, shrewd, persuasive, pleasing in manner and address, endowed with the gifts that win popularity; but he was vacillating. He was one of the kind whom we meet every day—vehement but variable. Men were drawn to him magnetically, but they had no security that the alliance would be lasting. He was perfectly sincere; he spoke the genuine sentiment which he entertained at the moment. But there was no guarantee that he would retain this sentiment at the end of the hour. There is a type of character which is described as slow but sure; Aaron might be portrayed as quick but uncertain.

AARON AND SIMON PETER

I have always regarded Aaron as the Simon Peter of the Old Testament. No two men separated by long centuries are more alike. Both were lovable; both were outspoken; both were rapid in resolution; both received a call in advance of their brethren; both performed deeds of the most jealous service; and both on certain occasions were singularly untrue to their first impulse.

I will add one parallel more—both were the founders of a ministry. Of Aaron, as of Peter, it was virtually said, "On this rock I will build my church." Aaron, like Peter, received the key of a new dispensation; he was placed as head pastor over the congregation of liberated Israel; church and state were, for the first time, separated in thought. One naturally asks, Why should Aaron have been fit for the church when he was not fit for the state? If he had not the qualities of a rock for politics, why should he have been credited with these qualities for the pastorate?

It is not suggested by the narrative that Moses promoted him to the priesthood in ignorance of his weak point. On the contrary, the most striking exhibition of that weakness occurred previous to his ordination. The incident may be briefly stated. Moses went up to the solitudes of Mount Sinai to commune with the God of Israel. Aaron was left in charge of the multitude on the plain. But the absence of the one man made the multitude lonely. Loneliness might help the religion of Moses; but it did harm to theirs. They craved a symbol, an image, something to represent God. Moses had been that symbol, that image, that representative. But Moses was gone. He had disappeared in the mountain mists; he might never return.

They came to Aaron to ask a sign—a visible monument of the Divine Presence. Aaron demurred. The crowd grew clamorous. They passed from request into murmur, from murmur into mutiny. Aaron yielded. He told them to bring their gold earrings, and from these combined treasures he constructed the image of a young bull, such as the Egyptians worshiped. He only meant it for an image; he told the crowd in so many words that it was intended to represent the God of Israel. But the crowd hailed it as the God of Egypt—the presence by which the pharaohs had prospered. They forgot their patriotism. They cried, in effect, "Let the Egyptian omen be our omen!" They broke into shouts of joy, but the shout of joy was a shout of rebellion.

Now this scene of tumult and uproar came from the vacillation of Aaron. He had manifested a spirit of accommodation, a tendency to move with the crowd. In contemplating the picture in the Gallery, my wonder has always been why Moses is represented in an attitude so lenient towards Aaron. We do not, indeed, associate Aaron with the rebellion of the crowd nor deem that he was worthy of their penalty. But Aaron is not only pardoned—he is promoted; he is raised to that position of eminence in the church which is denied him in the state. With the full knowledge of his vacillating spirit, with the full proof before the world that he had been guilty of compromise, this man is invested with the high priest's office, with the chief pastorate of the great congregation.

I am looking at the matter merely artistically—from the standpoint of a spectator in the Gallery. Keeping purely to the aesthetic, I ask, is it not a breach of art, a violation of the law of harmony, a dislocation in the proportion of things? What is the problem? It is this: a man rejected by the state as unfit to be a leader by reason of his vacillating spirit is by that same state selected to be the head of a religious community within its own pale! I have never found the Great Gallery defective in matters of proportion; I have never known the hand of its artists to apply inappropriate colors. But is there not such a misapplication here? Is there not in this picture an inartistic element, a breach of consistency which mars its beauty? We can understand that a stone once rejected should afterwards become the head of the corner provided its rejection were found to be a mistake; but that a stone should be made the head of the corner which was once rejected and which is still known to possess the defect attributed to it—this is surely a fault of the builder!

ACCOMMODATION TO CIRCUMSTANCES

But I think we have forgotten one thing of great importance—the difference of qualification requisite for a leader in the state and a leader in the church. The quality which would be a blemish in a rock is a beauty in a flower—tenderness. That a rock should be easily bent or broken is a proof of its unfitness; but that a rose should be easily bent or broken is an element in its charm. The simile has direct application here. The leader of a state ought to be unbending; firmness is essential to successful government. But the pastor in a congregation ought not to be unbending. His province is that of a servant. It is required before all things that he should be a man of human sympathy—able to adapt himself to the needs of each time.

The characteristic of the individual church leader and the characteristic of the church universal must always be one of accommodation to circumstances. That is the secret of Christianity's power. It has been durable amid shifting epochs just because it has been willing to assimilate these epochs. The stream has been content to take its color from the soil through which it flows; therefore it has irrigated many soils. It has turned its ear to the special needs of special ages. It has not granted all for which each crowd has clamored; but it has granted something—it has recognized that every widespread clamor implies a widespread want. It has met the cry for imperialism; it has met the cry for freedom; it has met the cry for asceticism; it has met the cry for earthly loveliness; it has met the cry for reconciliation between religion and science. This priesthood has conquered by stooping, has reigned by serving, has endured by veiling what is not essential to its faith. Its power of survival has been its power of accommodation.

Let me make a supposition. Let us imagine that the man selected to fill the high priest's office had been not Aaron but Joshua. A greater contrast than that between Aaron and Joshua cannot be conceived. If Aaron was vacillating, Joshua was unbending; if Aaron was soft, Joshua was inflexible. The future leader of the army of Israel was a man of no compromise. To him it was enough that the law had once been given; to be once given was to be enforced permanently. We know that on account of this quality Joshua was made head of the state; why was he not made head of the church? Though a little younger, he was contemporaneous with Aaron; he lived in the same environment; he was familiar with the same conditions of life. Why did the Gallery not select him as the pastor to the great congregation? Clearly because church and state require opposite types of mind. Joshua made a great leader of the army; he would have made a very poor leader of the church. The reason is that, while the army wants an absolute leader, the church does not.

The church leader must be content to be, in a measure, led. He must consent, in certain things, to follow. He must watch the course of the stream. He must observe the current of the time. He must consider the state of the tide. Aaron was chosen because he was such a man as that. No other type of mind but the bending mind will suit the church leader. Aaron erred not by his efforts at conciliation but by his means of conciliation; instead of making a golden calf, he should have told the clamoring crowd that they would soon have a visible tabernacle. His error was, after all, one of detail. The principle was misapplied, but it was good and true. The man who can feel the pulse of the multitude and suit his gospel to their needs is the man who merits the foremost place in the sphere of the pastoral office.

Aaron's Rod Blossomed

And this to my mind furnishes the explanation of an incident in the life of Aaron to which I think no other explanation has lent any significance. Twelve rod-branches of the almond tree are deposited in the tabernacle. Each rod represents a secular power; they stand respectively for the twelve heads of the twelve clans or tribes of Israel. To these rods another is added—making thirteen. The thirteenth is the rod of Aaron—representing the spiritual as distinct from the secular power. On the day after they have been placed in the tabernacle, Moses enters the building and finds a wonderful phenomenon. The twelve rods remain as they were when first deposited; but the thirteenth—the rod of Aaron—has burst forth into bloom.

Now, what is the ideal significance of this? To me it clearly means that in the tabernacle of God, in the sphere of the religious ministry, the forces which will survive are not the secular forces. None of the twelve rods of temporal power will flourish here. The very thing which makes them survivors in the world would kill them in the church—their inability to bend. They can bud in secular life, because the secular ruler reigns by the exercise of authority. But the spiritual life is not ruled by the exercise of authority. It is ruled by the veiling of authority—by sacrifice, by love. Only one rod will blossom here—the rod of Aaron! Only one power will bear fruit here—the power of stooping! Within this holy temple the laws of survival are altered, reversed! The things which once disqualified become the source of life; the rod which would in the outward kingdom have only served for firewood becomes, in the spiritual sphere, a scepter of potent power!

THE STRENGTH OF AARON

The strength of Aaron, then, is to lie in something which in the secular province would be called weakness—the capacity to be bent by the troubles of the crowd. We have a fine and a typical instance of this in the sixteenth chapter of Numbers, where Aaron is seen standing "between the dead and the living." He appears as the intercessor for stricken humanity. A dreadful plague has fallen—fallen as a vengeance. The anger of the God of Israel has been kindled, and thousands lie low beneath the stroke of the pestilence. Then follows a scene of sublime humanitarianism.

Aaron takes his place among the stricken and pours forth his prayer to heaven. He stands on the pestilential field whose atmosphere is reeking with contagion. In front of him are the

remaining members of the congregation who are still untouched—
trembling, cowering, anticipating. Behind him are the dying and
the dead—a ghastly concourse. Aaron is in that charnel house.
He stands on no hill apart from the multitude. He utters his
prayers from no palatial retreat securely embowered against the
entrance of infection. He comes down into the foul air, into the
vile miasma. He identifies himself with the case of the dead, of
the dying, of those who are preparing to die. His attitude is that
of a participator, of one who wishes to be numbered among the
transgressors. He could have been no coward to face the virulence
of a deadly and contagious malady! It throws a fresh light upon
his attitude toward the worshipers of the golden calf. We
commonly attribute that attitude to timorousness; it is more likely
to have been the fruit of pity! Was it not simply another phase of
humanitarian sympathy—that same humanitarian sympathy which
here prompts him in the hour of pestilence to take his stand
beside his stricken brethren?

And this has ever since been the characteristic note of the Bible
priesthood. In this sphere the rod of empire has habitually burst
into softness. The true priesthood has ever been a service of man;
every stage of its development has been a stooping further down.
Step by step it has descended into the depths of human care and
human sorrow. Step by step it has identified itself with the lot of
the suffering and the sinful, till it has reached the last valley of
humiliation at the cross of the Son of Man. Aaron did not, any
more than Moses, enter the land to which he was going. To both it
was only a promised land. Each had a mountain view of coming
glory; each died in the faith of a world to come. But to posterity
the world of each has come. The land whose dominion was prefigured to the eye of Moses has more than realized his dream; the
priesthood which floated before the sight of Aaron has attained a
grander goal than his fancy pictured. The brothers have each had
their reward, and each a reward after his kind. Moses bore the
secular scepter, and he has inherited the crown of Christendom;
the highest thrones of the world are built upon his Law. Aaron
bore the rod which blossomed into a passion-flower, and it has
issued in the Cross of Calvary; the climax of the heart's devotion
is the sacrifice of Jesus.

A PRAYER

Endow me, O Lord, with the priestly spirit; consecrate me to the service of Your tabernacle! Help me to take my place with the stricken sons of the wilderness! I do not ask to be enabled to pray for them on the height; let me come down from the height! Let me stand in the scene of the pestilence! Let me touch the lepers' spots before I say "Be thou clean!" Often have I thought of these words, "If a man be overtaken in a fault, restore him in the spirit of meekness."

I have seen those who would restore in the spirit of pride; they speak to the fallen, but they speak from the mountaintop. Not thus would I restore, O Lord. I would come with Christ down from my heaven; I would empty myself with Him. Let me descend with Him into the manger! Let me breathe the atmosphere of the beasts of the stall! Let me wrap myself in the humble garments of a child of earth! Let me join in the common struggle of the sons of Nazareth! Let me accept the same baptism that is offered to the vilest!

Teach me that for the healing of a soul there is more virtue in the touch than in the ointment! Let the touch precede the text; let the pity precede the precept; let the kindness precede the kingdom; let the brotherhood with man precede the breath of God! Let me meet the fallen in their own valley, the desolate in their own ruin, the broken in their own desert, the wandered in their own night! Then shall I be in truth one of Your royal priesthood.

For Further Study and Reflection

1. What does Matheson mean when he says that most people are neither outstanding successes nor total failures but simply at some point miss the mark?

2. How does a pastor/priest accommocate to the circumstances of his time?

3. What is the difference between speaking to the people from the scene of the pestilence and speaking from the mountaintop?

4. What is the strength of Aaron?

5. Compare and contrast a political leader with a religious leader.

11

CALEB THE EXPLORER

There is one respect in which the Jew has more resemblance to the Briton than to any other national group in the world—he has been a great colonist. He has been transplanted into lands the most diverse from his own, and he has flourished there. He has been carried into Egypt. He has been settled in Syria. He has been resident in Babylon. He has sojourned in Persia. He has been amalgamated with Greece. He has been a subject of Rome. He has been a dweller in all the lands of the West. In all these directions he has preserved his nationality, yet he has adapted himself to the new soil.

But if the Jew and the Briton resemble each other in their power of colonization, they resemble each other also in this, that with both of them the power of colonization has been an acquired thing. Neither the Jew nor the Briton has been, by nature, a geographical explorer. Both have had an original impulse to be self-contained, to keep within their own walls. Their motives have been different—that of Britain has been an insular prejudice, that of Judah has been a religious isolation. But in each case the effect has been the same—a tendency to shrink within the shell. In both instances the migration has been something thrust upon the nation against its will. The act has been salutary, but it has not been spontaneous; it has been the result of external influence.

THE JEWISH NATIONAL GOAL

Turning specifically to the Jew as he is historically exhibited in the Great Gallery, we are impressed with the fact that he is by nature the man of his own fireside and that he is called from that fireside only by outside voices. His is not naturally the instinct of the swallow—the instinct of migration. Doubtless he is ever stretching towards the future, but it is a national future. What he seeks is a brighter glow of his own fire. His goal is the coming of his Messiah, but his Messiah is not to take him out but to bring others in. He looks upon the Christ not as One who will transplant him into other lands, but as One who will transplant other lands into Jewish soil.

His motto has been ever "Home, sweet home." If he desired travel, it was not that he might explore but that he might export. He wanted to make every house a model of his own—the same in architecture, the same in furniture. He would have all things to be fashioned after the pattern of his own mount.

THE FIRST JEWISH EXPLORERS

It is this absence of a migratory instinct that makes the type of the explorer very rare in the Jewish Gallery. Take the Gallery of Genesis; I find there much locomotion but little voluntary migration. I see the primeval man leaving his first home, but he is compelled to it by the sweat of the brow. I see Cain quitting the sanctuary for a foreign land, but he is driven to it by the shadow of a crime. I see the family of Noah become emigrants, but they are borne on the waters of a flood. I see Jacob flying from his hearth, but it is fear that drives him. I see Joseph passing into Egypt, but it is not as a traveler—it is as a captive.

In all the Gallery of Genesis I behold but one voluntary emigrant—the man Abraham. He alone receives an impulse of the heart to leave his country and his kindred and his father's house in search of other shores. Yet, even with him, exploration is hardly the motive. He is rather the missionary than the traveler. He goes not forth to seek information but to impart it. It is no curiosity that prompts him; it is pity. He desires not a better country but a better light for other countries. The one voluntary emigrant in the Gallery of Genesis is not a merchant man seeking goodly pearls but one who has already found a pearl of great price and who longs to reveal it to the sons of other lands.

It is when the Gallery begins to exhibit the scenes of the desert that we catch the first trace of the spirit of exploration. In the heart of the wilderness of Paran we see a band of men animated by an impulse unfamiliar to eastern climes—the impulse of the traveler. While India and China remain at home, while Egypt sits down beside her own pyramids, while Babylon suns herself in the glories she has gathered, this humble desert tribe proposes to explore.

CALEB THE EXPLORER

Abraham had gone forth without knowing whither he went; he had been content thus to go. He had been in the position of a man who says, "I will not take lodgings in advance; I shall trust, when I arrive, to find vacant rooms." But here in the desert of Paran there steps forth a man who says, "I intend to walk on a different basis; I must know beforehand whither I am traveling." That man is Caleb, the son of Jephunneh.

Caleb is the type of the explorer—the first type in the Great Gallery of the traveler—as distinct from the missionary. He is a member of the earliest geographical society. It had twelve members in all. Their names have been preserved, but none have become immortal with the exception of two—Joshua and Caleb. I think Caleb was here the leader. Joshua was rather an actor than an investigator. He was more for the camp than for the council, more for the hour than for the outlook.

But Caleb had something of Moses in him. He had an eye for the future. He was capable of Pisgah glimpses. He was one of those lives who seem always to be pitched upon a hill; he could see things afar off. He is the real hero of this enterprise; he has made the work of exploration his own. Joshua is the actual conqueror of Canaan; Caleb is the man who predicted the advantage of possessing it.

MOSES' SPEECH

In the depths of the desert of Paran Moses addressed this geographical society. What he said in effect was this: "You are now within measurable distance of that land of Canaan which has been the heaven of your dreams and of the dreams dreamt by your fathers. You are within range of that country to which you have looked forward as to a second paradise, which is to compensate you for the Eden you have lost.

"The time has come when it will be well for you to consider

whether the reality will correspond to the dream. It may be that your ideal of glory is not the ideal of glory entertained by your fathers. It may be that the lifting of the veil from this land of promise will reveal it to be what you have not pictured, what you have not desired. Consider well before you take possession of that which you know not. Examine carefully that ground which you are eager to colonize. Go up and inspect it beforehand. Walk round its bulwarks and study its buildings. Mark the life of its inhabitants and the pursuits of its citizens. Enquire whether your desert troubles are likely to die within its walls, whether you will be allowed to drop your burdens when you enter within its gates. Take heed lest your colony be a calamity, your heaven a heaviness, your promised land a permanent loss!"

I believe this to be the real significance of the speech of Moses. On any other view we are confronted by a difficult problem. Why should Moses have sent out Caleb and his comrades to explore a land to which the finger of God was pointing? Did not the pointing of that Divine hand dispense with the need of any exploration? Had not God Himself prepared the land? Why commission Caleb and his companions to inquire whether a colony could be planted there? According to the narrative, there never was a doubt on that matter.

The entrance of the people was secured whenever they should go up—secured by the promise of God. Their whole march had been a march of faith. Their ability to enter the Promised Land had never been based upon human resources; was it to be based upon human resources now? Their hope that the gates of Canaan would open to let them in had always rested on the Word of the Lord; was it now, for the first time, to rest on the word of Jizan? Was faith to drop her wings at the very gate of paradise? Was trust to become bankrupt within sight of the city of gold? Was the confidence of getting admission into the Promised Land, which had originally reposed in the fact of the promise, to seek its anchorage on a totally different shore—the explorations of a geographical society?

THE DESIRABILITY OF ENTRANCE TO THE PROMISED LAND

That, I say, is the problem which naturally arises. But, if you take the speech of Moses as I have paraphrased it, things will appear in another light. For, as I take it, the question before the geographical society was not the *possibility* of getting an entrance into Canaan; it was the *desirability* of getting that entrance. The land was ready for the people; were the people ready for the land? Were they morally developed in a sufficient degree to enter upon their birthright? Had they attained mental maturity? Could they appreciate as yet their coming destiny? Granting that Canaan was a city of gold, a city of gold is not the ideal of a child; it would prefer a city of tinsel or a city of fireworks.

The exploring expedition was really an exploration of the mind; geographical in form, it was spiritual in import. Its goal was self-examination. The report which Caleb and his comrades were to bring was to decide not a question of geography but a question of philosophy. It was to test the present capacity of the people of God, to determine whether the heart of Israel was ripe for its inheritance.

The truth is, the children of Israel as described in the Great Gallery, are related to the physical Canaan very much as Emanuel Swedenborg felt himself related to the Christian heaven. To Swedenborg the question never was whether a man would get into a special physical locality. He had, as I interpret him, no doubt whatever that, so far as mere space was concerned, the good and the bad would occupy the same position—stand by the same crystal river, gaze on the same pure fountain. It was their spiritual localities that were to differ. Standing on the same spot, they were to be oppositely affected; the pure eye was to see beauty, the impure eye was to read deformity. I am no Swedenborgian, but I have always felt that he has here touched a profound Christian thought.

In one of the parables of Christ there is introduced a remarkable conception. There is pictured a man who has actually succeeded in getting into heaven. He has entered among the guests bidden to the King's table. So far as admission is concerned, he has passed the Rubicon and secured the prize. But on his admission, his troubles only begin. They originate in the fact that he has not the adequate robe—that his own personality is defective. He is unfit for his environment, unsuited to his surroundings; that which vibrates to others with the joy of wedding bells reverberates like a dirge to him. Swedenborg, doubtless, had this passage in his mind when he formed his conception of heaven.

WAS ISRAEL READY FOR CANAAN?

Even such was the conception entertained by Moses of the physical Canaan. He had no doubt whatever that Israel would get in. The question in his mind was, what would she do when she did get in? Would she find her ideal realized? Was she ready for the destined land? Was she sufficiently grown to participate in its pursuits? Ought not she to have a preliminary test applied—a test not of the land's beauty but of her own ripeness? Let her destiny be spread before her. Let her have a glimpse of that country of which she had dreamed. By her acceptance or by her refusal of the proffered cup would it be known assuredly whether she had reached maturity.

Therefore it was that Caleb and his band went up—twelve chosen apostles sent to explore the coming heaven. They were not chosen on spiritual grounds; that would have been to deprive the test of all value. The object was to determine what the average mind would think—not what would be the judgment of the elite. In point of fact, there were only two superior minds among them—Caleb and Joshua; out of any twelve taken at random, you will seldom get more than that.

Now, I have often put to myself an imaginary problem. Let us suppose that twelve men were divinely selected to have a preliminary vision of the Christian heaven with the object of reporting its nature to their fellowmen. Let us suppose that to make them representative of their fellowmen the selection was made without reference to spirituality and wholly on the ground of investigative powers. The question I put is this, What would be the probable result of such an exploring expedition? And I think the answer must be that there would not be found more than two out of the twelve who would approve the vision.

SACRIFICE AT THE CENTER OF LIFE IN CANAAN

It is almost certain that at the sight of the Christian heaven ten of the company would start back in dismay—not appalled by the difficulty but appalled by the facility of getting in. For they would see there the last thing they expected to see—a life of sacrifice at the center. Whatever grapes of Eshcol they might behold, whatever gates of pearl they might gaze on, whatever streets of gold they might survey, they would always recognize behind these objects the presence of that form which they had regarded as the symbol of misery—the Cross. The skies of the nightless paradise would be obscured by the shadow of God, and all the music and dancing would not induce them to go in!

Now, this is the actual position of the twelve explorers of the physical Canaan. They came to the land of their dreams; they entered within the gates; they stood spectators of the scene. And in presence of that scene ten of their number grew faint with dismay. They had pictured something different, something opposite. They had expected luxurious ease, voluptuous rest. Here in the very interior of Canaan was a vision of sacrifice—the image of a Cross!

The land which they had deemed the home of luxury revealed the prospect of long and arduous labor, of struggle with alien powers, of burdens by night and day! It was altogether the reverse of what they had pictured in their fancy. Instead of minimizing their cares, it promised to increase their cares, to add to their weights, to intensify their contact with pain. The effect was immediate and disastrous; the ten refused the prize. Only two of the twelve explorers were willing to make trial of their heaven—Joshua and Caleb. Of these, I think, Caleb was the more eager. Joshua had many great days to come; I think this was Caleb's special day.

CALEB'S STAND

Joshua can claim his Gibeon and his Jericho and his passage of Jordan, but this little spot is Caleb's own. It is his one laurel wreath, his bloodless, his unobtrusive triumph. Bloodless though it is, it is a grand victory. We see a man standing up in almost solitary protest against the cry for regress. We see a man trying to convince his disheartened comrades that they are abandoning solid gold, that the country they despise is really a scene of promotion. It is a noble spectacle; nonetheless noble because to these comrades, to that generation, Caleb's call was vain.

Another generation was to justify him, to join him; for the present, the voices of the ten outweighed the voices of the two.

When the people received the report of the majority and found that report to be bad, they cried with loud voice that they would not go. It was in vain that Caleb pointed to the grapes he had gathered at Eshcol; it was in vain he tried to tempt his countrymen. Caleb was before his time—forty years before his time. The light he expected from the morning was to fall on his declining days, but the morning and the midday were to be spent in hope deferred. The man who could keep his hope burning when the torches of the million were extinguished is entitled to be called one of God's heroes.

MEN OF SACRIFICE

There are in the field of speculation two opposite classes of men whom we equally associate with the idea of sacrifice—those whom an age thrusts prematurely forward and those whom an age steadily keeps back. As the type of the former, I would take King Saul; he was the victim of a premature passion conceived by his race—the desire to have a king. But the type of the latter is Caleb, and he has a still larger representation. He stands for a very wide constituency which has its members in all lands and in all times.

There is no sphere of history in which you will not meet with that phenomenon—the man who is kept back by his generation. The figure of Caleb, first seen in the desert of Paran, meets us again and again as the ages roll. We see him at ever recurring periods looking out upon the sea of life and discerning in the blue expanse islands which other eyes cannot perceive. We hear him calling out to his fellows, "Come and let us explore this new region of the earth; give me ships, give me money, give me men!" But ever the answer is the same, "We see no islands there; we behold no sphere for enterprise—nothing but the waste of waters, nothing but the ocean waves." Caleb is deemed under a delusion—the island is only in his eye; the land of which he dreams exists but in his heart. Caleb has to bear in silence the burden of his weight of glory.

In all that generation of disappointed Israel the man most to be pitied was the man whose ideal was not broken. I think, in looking at this picture, we bestow our compassion in the wrong quarter. We center our pity on that generation of Israel which shut against themselves the gates of their earthly paradise. But I think the real object for commiseration is the man whom they shut out in shutting out themselves. Caleb is the tragedy of the play; the exclusion of the multitude is in one sense its comedy. That thousands of men, on the adverse report of a geographical committee, should voluntarily turn away from the heaven of their dreams is a conception in which there is something grotesque. But the spectacle of that crowd holding back a man who desires to enter in, the spectacle of an individual life debarred from the enjoyment of his paradise by the simple fact that his comrades are not ripe for the same heaven—this is something more allied to tears than to laughter.

The one thing which dries the tears is the sublime spirit of sacrifice which lies beneath it. Caleb acquiesces in the postponement of his own heaven. A Christian apostle says that he would be content to be accursed for the sake of his brethren. Caleb is at all events content to step down for the sake of his brethren. He takes without a murmur the lower room—the room where his brothers dwell. He consents, during forty years, to wear a garb inferior to his own—a garb which associates him with the rank of souls far beneath him. He accepts without complaining the command to seek the vale. He conceals his aspiration. He hides his contempt for the sordid throng. He gives no hint that he is above their business. He joins them on their own level, in their own work. He never tells his love; he buries his sorrow. He takes up his brothers' cares—cares about inferior things. He puts his hand to the duties of the desert when his heart is up in Canaan. Like a greater than himself, he turns his eye from the opened heavens to contemplate the fact that there is no bread in the wilderness.

The Crowd Looks Backward

Regarding that crowd in the desert which had shut against themselves the door of Canaan, there is one point in the picture which has often struck me. They refuse to enter Canaan, but they never dream of remaining in the desert. The alternative in their minds is not between going forward and standing still; it is between going forward and traveling back. If they demur to go on, it is not that they may encamp but that they may retreat. As the ideal of the future disappears, there rises the ideal of the past; their cry is, "Let us get back to Egypt!" They call for a new leader—a leader whose watchword shall be, not "advance," but "retire." The glories of hope have faded; they resolve to glorify memory. The sun of fancy has ceased to light the hills of Canaan; they will try to kindle it on the plains of Egypt. Egypt, while a present experience, had been the reverse of a glory; but, when the light faded from the future, the past caught a fictitious glow. It is ever thus.

When our prospect of the evening becomes overcast, we gild with glory the memory of our morning sky. In no circumstances can man dwell in the present; curtain his Canaan, and he will fly back to Egypt. You and I cannot live in the hour; if we are not to go forward, we must go back. Our alternatives are hope or memory, Canaan or Egypt, the land of promise or the land of retrospect. The intermediate spot is ever desert—a barren waste. Thought cannot dwell there, never seeks to dwell there. It must have either wings for tomorrow or wings for yesterday; it must "fly away" if it would be at rest.

A PRAYER

Be mine, then, the wings for tomorrow, my God! If I get first the wings for tomorrow, I shall then be able to go back. Memory cannot bring hope, but hope can adorn memory—even dark memory. Seen from the hills of Canaan, Egypt may seem very beautiful; its toils may be glorified, its pains may be justified. If You are preparing me for a heaven of sacrificial love, these toils, these pains, are already justified. If my Canaan were a mere pleasure ground, every tear shed in Egypt would be a waste of time.

But when, like Caleb, I look through the crystal bars of Your city and see that the Cross is the crown thereof, I understand it all. I understand why Your roses have been red, not white. I understand why drops of blood have strewn life's garden. I understand why my will has so often been thwarted, why my schemes have so often miscarried, why my road has so often been interrupted. It is because Your land of Canaan is a land of sacrifice, and I am preparing for that sacrifice.

It is because the rose of Your heaven is the passion flower of

Calvary. It is because the center of Your throne holds a Lamb that was slain. It is because the messengers of Your will are ministering spirits. It is because Your resurrection life keeps the print of the nails. It is because the lowliest are the greatest in the kingdom of Your glory. The bondage of Egypt will be a golden memory when I accept the vision of Your land of Canaan.

For Further Study and Reflection

1. What is different about Caleb as an explorer as compared to the earlier men who left their homes?

2. What was at the heart of Moses' speech in the desert of Paran?

3. Why did conquering Canaan represent a life of sacrifice rather than a life of ease?

4. How was Caleb a man ahead of his time? Who are some other examples of this type of person in history?

5. Why did the Israelites' refusal to enter Canaan become a cry to return to Egypt?

12

BOAZ THE KIND

The representative men of an age are not necessarily the great men. Greatness is certainly one of the permanent things in humanity, but it is far from being the only permanent thing. Through the ages human nature keeps not only its mountains but also its valleys and its plains. Any gallery of representative men which professes to be adequate must include with the hills the plains and valleys too. Genius is eternal, but so is gentleness. Masterminds are ever recurring but so are minds of ordinary mold.

There is a gold which glitters not, which shines not in history, but which is none the less a permanent possession of man; it is that species of gold which belongs to life's beaten path and dusty way. I have often been struck with the words of Paul in depicting the attributes of love. He applies to it both a telescope and a microscope. When he looks through the telescope, he cries, "Love beareth, believeth, hopeth, endureth all things." But when he takes up the microscope, he sees that love is equally unfading in its minutest forms, and he expresses this in the words, "Love is kind."

In looking at this Bible Gallery I have asked myself the question, Is there any figure which represents pure and simple kindness? There are many poetic qualities represented; Enoch has his walk with God and Moses his glimpse of faith and David his gift of song. There are many solid qualities represented. Noah has his power of exhortation and Joshua his power of serving and Job his power of waiting and Isaac his power of obeying.

But is there no place for a quality which is neither poetic nor solid—the power of simple kindness? Is there no place for that quality which cannot manifest itself by flights nor yet reveal itself by mechanical movement on the ground but which exists merely as a still small voice in the heart? I feel that there ought to be such a place, that without it no gallery of portraits can represent humanity. Where shall we look for this lowly form? Where in this Bible Gallery shall we find a picture which is dedicated to the homely attribute of kindness? All the portraits we have yet surveyed are on a large scale. Adam holds the fate of humanity, Noah the fate of a world, Abraham the fate of a kingdom—the spheres are all too important for mere goodheartedness. Can we meet with any spot in the whole portraiture sufficiently limited in its range and sufficiently humble in its scope to furnish the theater for a life of unobtrusive kindness?

THE TENDER HEART OF BOAZ

Now, there is one such portrait in the Great Gallery. It is that of Boaz of Bethlehem. He is distinguished from all the others by the unique smallness of the sphere in which he dwells. He fills a very narrow niche, but it is a niche that otherwise would be unfilled. He represents but one quality, but nowhere in the Gallery is that quality represented so perfectly. He is distinctively the man of kindness. This is his abiding glory; by nothing else does he live in memory.

The men of his day would have valued him for something impersonal. From a worldly point of view he had many advantages. He was of good family. He had great social influence. He was possessed of much wealth. He belonged to a tribe which was already beginning to take the lead in Israel. But by none of these things does this man endure. Their remembrance is only kept alive by the remembrance of another quality which his contemporaries would have passed by—the possession of a tender heart.

BOAZ'S KINDNESS IS SEEN IN SMALL TASKS

More than any one I know within the compass of the Old Testament, Boaz survives by "the grand old name of gentleman." The nearest approach to him in the New, among those reputed merely human, is Barnabas. Boaz, like Barnabas, was a "son of consolation." He was so, without trying to be so—by the sheer force of that quality which for want of a better name we designate "good nature." He did not aim at being kind, did not recognize that he was kind. He was so innate a gentleman that he knew it not. Like Moses, "he knew not that the skin of his face shone." His countenance was veiled to his own goodness. He was one of those who, if commended for his charities, would have used the words of surprise put into the mouth of the saints at the Day of Judgment, "Lord, when saw I You hungry or thirsty or sick and ministered to You?" Kindness was to him as natural as to a bird its song.

The most striking feature in this kindness of Boaz is the apparently trivial nature of the things in which it showed itself. It was not in large donations; it was not in heroic sacrifices. It was in things so small as to seem unworthy of record. Strange as it may sound to say so, I think it is this seeming triviality of sphere that brings Boaz nearest to the Christian standard. According to that standard it is the smallest sphere which most conclusively proves a man, "He that is faithful in that which is least, is faithful also in much" (Luke 16:10). We often hear the phrase, "a Christian gentleman." What is a Christian gentleman?

A Christian Gentleman

Wherein does a gentleman of the school of Christ differ from a gentleman of the mere worldly school? I have no hesitation in saying that the difference lies in their comparative power of descending into minute things. It is the difference between law and grace. There is a law of etiquette as well as a law of Moses— a social code which the man of the world must not transgress. But he may refuse to transgress this code and still be outside the Christian standard. The Christian standard goes down below law. It does more than the book of etiquette commands, more than is taught in the world's school.

The Christian gentleman, as much as the Christian saint, is justified by grace not law. He would not be satisfied with keeping any set of social commandments. His authority is derived not from Sinai but from Calvary—not from any conventional code but from the dictates of the individual heart.

Now, Boaz is a gentleman of the heart—not of the salon. He does things not only which the salon would not demand but which the salon might forbid. His attitude to his dependents is remarkable. When he goes to his daily work, he salutes his servants with what would now be called a shaking of hands. His first greeting to his reapers is not the voice of the master to the employed but the voice of the well-wisher to his friends. He comes into the field and says, "The Lord be with you!" And from a hundred lips and hearts the response comes forth, "The Lord bless you!" That is a relationship which goes beyond etiquette. It is outside the boundaries of all law; it is pure grace or, what is here the same thing, graciousness.

It is a relationship which is founded on the principle, "Be a man first and an employer afterwards." It starts with the recognition not of subordination but of equality. It realizes the agreement beneath the difference, the unity underlying the separation. In an age when the gulf between master and servant was more marked than it is now, the reciprocal greeting of Boaz and his reapers meets us like an oasis in the social Sahara.

Boaz First Encounters Ruth

But the crowning glory of Boaz appears in his treatment of one individual life—the fair and gentle Ruth. It is she that has made his name immortal. All his wealth and all his property would not have saved him from oblivion if he had not stooped in kindness to that young woman. The difficulty is to tell the story with adequate simplicity.

As told by the painting in the Old Gallery, it is a tale sublimely artless, charmingly unadorned. It leaves on the mind the impression of one who is depicting something the beauty of which he does not know. There is no striving for effect, no contemplation of effect. The scene is displayed prosaically, mechanically. Yet the result is high poetry—idyllic poetry. It is a picture of ideal virtue in the midst of surrounding debasement, of primitive purity in an age of artificial sins. It is a daisy planted on a granite rock; it is Jacob resting on a pillow of stone; it is a pearl reposing in the depths of a stormy sea.

One afternoon, when the reapers had finished their work, Boaz came into his field to survey the result of their labor. His eye lighted on a fair girl gleaning the fragments that remained. She was doubtless meanly clad; in any case, the act bespoke her poverty. Yet the fine eye of Boaz detected beneath the folds of the mantle the light of better days. "Who is that?" he asks. They answer, "It is a young woman from Moab who married a son of one of your kinsmen—Elimelech of Judah."

"What has brought her here?" he asks. They tell him that she has become a widow and has left her own land through love of her widowed mother-in-law, Naomi. Here was rather a startling piece of news for a rich and respectable proprietor in the land of Israel! He finds himself to be kinsman to a young woman who is an object of charity in his own field and earns a livelihood through the kindness of his workmen. She is a native, also, of a foreign country, a heathen country, a country which in the traditions of the past had never been friendly to his people.

Moab had been the eyesore of Israel. It had blocked her passage through the desert. It had given her its solemn malediction. It had leagued against her with Midian. It had proved a grave to her lawgiver, Moses. Was it now to corrupt her laboring men? Were not the women of Moab proverbially lascivious? Was not this new importation into his field a thing not to be tolerated? Did not personal pride and national principle alike counsel him to stand haughtily aloof from this woman and treat the tie of kindred as an unacknowledged bond?

BOAZ'S COMPASSION FOR RUTH

So Boaz might well have thought, so ninety men out of every hundred would have thought. But Boaz was one of the superior ten. He resolved to speak to this gleaner. He did speak to her; and his first favorable impression was strengthened. His feeling towards her took the form of a protector, a father. He forgot that he was a landed proprietor, a rich man, a man of high connection; he became simply a man. He was filled with compassion for the stranger. He ceased to dread that she would corrupt the reapers; he feared that the reapers would corrupt her.

With almost feminine insight he provided a safeguard. "Stand fast by my maidens," he says; in other words, he surrounds her with a cordon of young female companions on whose wholesome influence he can rely. In that moment and by that act he became one of the moderns. He was, unconsciously to himself, the inaugurator of a principle—a principle which, after lying underground for long centuries, was in the fullness of time to burst into flower and fruit.

I said in the previous chapter that Caleb might be called the founder of geographical societies. I think Boaz has the distinction of being the founder of another class of societies. The institution which Caleb founded was intended to stimulate young men to explore. But the institution which Boaz inaugurated had a converse object; it was meant to deter young women from exploring too soon. It was designed to keep the female heart as long as possible from a knowledge of the darker shades of life. It is that form of seminary which in modern days is called sometimes a Girls' Friendly Society, sometimes a Female Guild, sometimes a Young Women's Christian Association. We will not discuss the name; under all names the thing described is the same. The need felt by Boaz is the need felt by the twentieth century.

Ruth's Purity Needs Wholesome Society

The ancient Jew and the modern Briton have alike perceived that even the purest individual life cannot begin the world in isolation. Before both the same problem looms. Young Ruth is coming into the world's field, and the reapers are not yet the angels. What is to be done with her—so simple, so artless, so confiding? Shall we allow her to take her chance in the big field—with its nonangelic reapers? Shall no attempt be made to receive her into everlasting habitations? Among the many mansions of this world—which are not identical with the mansions of the Father's house—shall no one say to this damsel, "I am the place prepared for you"?

And the answer given to the question by modern Britain has been the answer given by ancient Israel—"Stand fast by my maidens!" Before entering the town, Ruth has been met at the gates—met by a band of sisters—and cared for. If our age is morally better than the age of our fathers, the change must in no small degree be referred to this cause. It is a question of high importance whether good or evil shall get the start, for it is often the start that in life decides the race. In the case of Ruth the

Gleaner, the influence of the Girls' Society was visible and powerful; she was kept pure; she walked sedately.

Perhaps it may seem that in her case I have attributed too much to the society, too little to her own past. I may be reminded that according to the picture in the Gallery, hers had always been a soul of burning love. Had she not manifested the most romantic sacrifice? Had she not left country, kindred, and home to obey the dictates of an impulse of the heart? Was this a woman who would be likely to go wrong? Was this one who required the aid of a Girls' Friendly Society? Would not her path in life have been amply secured without the intervention of Boaz?

THE DANGER OF RUTH'S ROMANTIC NATURE

But I think the danger of Ruth lay just in that romantic element of her nature which had driven her from her native land. Who are those women that are most apt to go morally astray? Is it the cold, the phlegmatic, the passionless? No, it is the women of strong impulse, of fervent feeling, of impassioned enthusiasm. There is a form of evil which tempts not the bad but the good, which appeals to that part of our nature seemingly the most unselfish. The light which leads astray appears, as the poet says, to be "light from heaven." We feel that a colder heart, a more selfish heart, would have been exempt from this temptation, would not have experienced this special form of Satan in the wilderness.

It was Ruth's romantic impulse that made her an object of solicitude. The woman who in the face of home and kindred could say to Naomi, "Where thou goest I will go, and where thou lodgest I will lodge," was capable of braving all conventions if an inner fire were kindled. The spectator in the Gallery feels that the Girls' Friendly Society is no accident of the picture.

BOAZ AS THE CENTER OF THE DRAMA

The truth is, I differ somewhat as to the common literary judgment on the book of Ruth. The prevailing view regards Ruth herself as the Hamlet of the piece. This is not my opinion. To me the center of the drama is Boaz. If he is a homely figure, it is because he is homelike—modern. Homely as he is, he is the real turning point of the drama. It is he that averts the danger from the Moabitess. No peril had ever befallen Ruth equal to that which beset her as a gleaner in the field. She was nearer the verge of calamity then than at any past period. Neither her widowhood nor her poverty nor her exile revealed so impending a cloud as hovered over her amid the cornfields of Bethlehem.

What Ruth needed was a protector—a tower of refuge. She found one. Boaz was the man for the hour, the only man that would have suited the hour. He brought to her the one thing she required—protective kindness. On no other bridge could we have trusted her to cross the Rubicon. There are services for which great qualities do not avail, which need the touch of a lowly hand. No brilliant figure could have been so artistic for the place and time, no image of beauty could have so graced the picture as does the image of this homely and unadorned man with the heart of human kindness.

And so the master and the gleaner met daily among the golden sheaves, and step by step their mutual interest grew. On her side, gratitude deepened; on his, tenderness increased. You will read wrongly the story of Boaz if you think that his kindness to Ruth came from a preliminary passion; it would be more correct to say that his passion came from a preliminary kindness. His first interest in her was a humanitarian interest; it was such as he would have felt to anyone similarly circumstanced. Nor do I think it is correct to say, as is popularly said in such cases, that his protective kindness gave place to another feeling. The love which came into his heart was no other feeling; it was but an intensifying of the first impression. Love's forms are varied; in this sphere, as in others, "whatsoever a man soweth that shall he also reap."

Love's Varieties

There are as many different kinds of love as there are different kinds of character. There is a love which is impulsive and vehement—which takes its kingdom by violence and will brook no delay. There is a love which is sober and practical—which expends its treasures not in words but in deeds; it is more concerned about the feeding than about the anointing, more occupied with the essentials than with the spices. There is a love which is intrinsically a state of friendship; it is founded on mutual sympathy and based on a community of ideas. And there is a love which is before all things maternal—which, whether it exists in mother or father or brother, is distinctly protective in character. All of these are produced by the respective natures which reveal them.

Now, the love felt by Boaz was a maternal love. He was a man with a mother's heart, and he took Ruth into that heart. He gave her that form of affection which belonged to his nature—the overflowing kindness of a large soul. The pastoral which began in tears closes in the sound of wedding bells.

It is a remarkable marriage; it is the marriage of Moab and Israel. I do not think an artist would have dared to invent such a picture. A marriage of Moab and Israel was a marriage of the Gentile and the Jew. Such a union was beyond the imagination of later times. A novelist of the days of Esther who ventured to conceive such a thought would have been treated as an outcast and an alien. A poet of the days of Josiah who embodied such a thought in words would have been greeted with the cursing of the land.

It was only in an age previous to the consolidation of Jewish ideas that the possibility of such a marriage could have been contemplated. Through all the subsequent history of Israel, Moab remained her most stubborn foe. Conquered by David, held for a brief space by his successors, wrested even in the hour of its bondage, it broke away from the yoke in the days of Ahab and returned to its chain no more. It was the permanent symbol of all that was antagonistic to Israel; the last thought which would naturally have suggested itself was the nuptial tie.

THE MARRIAGE OF MOAB AND ISRAEL

Yet, according to the Bible Gallery, this marriage was the very making of Israel. It was the germ cell from which her glory sprang. From this marriage came the splendor of the house of Judah; from this marriage came the line of David; from this marriage, at the end of the line, came a greater than David. Looking at the matter merely from the side of art, it is well worthy of consideration.

Why is it that from the very beginning there is admitted into this Jewish Gallery an element of Gentile blood? This much we can say, that it is this early union of the Gentile and the Jew that alone makes the Gallery consistent with itself. It is by the primitive germ cell that I understand the latest growth. The latest growth is the human soul of Jesus. It is, by the admission of those not His disciples, a soul in which are combined the religious fervor of the Jew and the intellectual freedom of the Gentile.

Where did Jesus get that union? From above? No, this is a phase of the human—not the Divine. From David? Doubtless—David's was a many-sided life. But where did David get it? The problem is only driven further back. There must have been an admixture of blood of which David was himself the offspring. We are driven back to the marriage bells of early Bethlehem—those marriage bells of Ruth and Boaz, of Moab and Israel, which proclaimed the primitive union of the Gentile and the Jew.

And so the birth hour of Israel as a nation originated in an act of kindness. It came from no mightier source, from no more potent evolution. Doubtless the contemporaries of Boaz would regard him as not within the range of practical politics. They would look upon him as a very useful man—good for benevolent subscriptions and estimable for acts of charity but too homely in his deeds to be a maker of history. Their eye would rest upon other and more noisy forms—great public speakers, great statesmen, great warriors. How completely has their judgment been reversed!

History has passed by all the loud forms. It has left behind in obscurity the magnates of the time—the speakers, the statesmen, the warriors. It has taken up the homeliest deed of the homeliest man and made it immortal. It has chosen the most modest flower of all the garden. It has planted the empire of Israel on a deed of lovingkindness and a thought of tender mercy. The last has been first; the humblest has been exalted. The kingdom which culminated in the Rose of Sharon has found its beginning in the Lily of the Valley.

A PRAYER

Plant in my garden, O Lord, this Lily of Kindness! I often neglect it for more attractive appearing flowers. I seek the red rose of a great sacrifice—something which will reveal the shedding of blood. I say, "If I could be a missionary, if I could give my life for Your cause, that would be something You could accept; but I have neither the fire nor the wood nor the lamb for such an offering." And so I fold my hands in impotence.

Yet all the time there is a field in front of my own door where I can find a larger sacrifice. Ruth is gleaning there—young, helpless, poor. Ruth is gleaning there—with a heavy heart and a drooping spirit. Ruth is gleaning there—beset with temptations on every side. I shall get no glory in helping her? It will add nothing to my name. Just there lies the sacrifice, O my Father!

Your flower for me is the Lily of the Valley. The world prizes it not; it is a flower that makes no garlands for the great—it is simply kindness. But after many days it will adorn Your garland. Ruth will reign by the kind word spoken; Ruth will revive by the kind deed done. The bread I have given will be her bread of life; the water I have given will be her water of life; the joy I have given will be her staff of life. My valley shall be exalted; my lily shall be lit with the morning sun; my touch of tenderness shall be transmitted to generations still unborn. I shall find my song of welcome in the music of the future. Inspire my heart, O Lord, for its yet humble strain!

For Further Study and Reflection

1. Why does Matheson call Boaz's love a maternal love?
2. How was Boaz's act of kindness a cause of greatness?
3. What is significant in the marriage of Moab and Israel?
4. How was Ruth helped by the association with other young women in Boaz's fields?
5. According to Matheson, did Boaz fall in love with Ruth "at first sight"?

13

GIDEON THE HUMBLE

The scientist tells us that in the world of physical nature there is always the same amount of force existing throughout the whole. There is never a diminution; there is never an increase; the sum of natural energy is the same yesterday and today and forever. It is my opinion that in the moral world there exists an analogous law. We speak of some ages as ages of brilliancy, of others as ages of spiritual dearth. When we are referring to the individual lives of men, the distinction is quite legitimate. But I believe that the sum of moral energy in the mass of humanity at any given age is the same. It is not a difference of quantity but a difference of distribution.

There are, I think, two typical periods recurring throughout the history of man—the age of crowning heights and the age of unbroken plains. The former is the period of great men—the time when vast energies are concentrated in individual breasts. The latter is the time when humanity is very much upon one level—when no record exists of present achievements or of contemporary men rising above their fellows.

Take, for example, the history of England. Compare the reign of Elizabeth with the period of Richard III. Popularly speaking, the former is an age of spiritual life, and the latter a time of spiritual deadness. In reality, they are both equally living, but their life is differently distributed. In Elizabeth's days the larger share is absorbed by a remarkable row of figures—the Shakespeares, the Bacons, the Marlowes, the Fords, the

Massingers, the Drakes, the Cecils. In the time of Richard, on the other hand, no individual is spiritually very rich, but the share of each is evenly divided over the mass, and it may be that the mass itself is on a higher scale.

THE GREAT MEN OF THE BOOK OF JUDGES

There is an age depicted in the Bible which is essentially the period of great men. It is the record of that time embraced in the narrative of the book of Judges. I do not mean that the men of that book are especially great; I mean that their greatness is especially utilized. None of them approaches Abraham or Moses or Joshua. But neither Abraham nor Moses nor Joshua is an isolated life; each moves in sympathy with his clan; his life is the life of his tribe. Far otherwise is it with the judges of Israel. They are men selected out of the mass to initiate a movement to which the mass is inadequate. Abraham, Moses, and Joshua are each the product of a previous civilization. But the judges of Israel have to make their civilization.

The divine call comes to each judge at a time of national collapse and summons each from among lapsed masses. Each has to go forth at first alone—to create his own world. He has to awake the sleeping multitude, to rouse the dormant energies of his countrymen, to kindle into life the smoldering embers of an ancient fire. When we speak of the evolutionary growth of nations, we are apt to forget the individual leaves in the process. We are apt to ignore the fact that there are flowers in many a prairie which by a quickened development spring up in a single night. We are apt to lose sight of the truth that there are ages in which the prominent factors are not laws, not principles, not processes but men—men who have suddenly been stimulated to take the initiative in a new movement and the plunge in a new sea. Such is the age described as the reign of Israel's judges.

GIDEON'S REPRESENTATIVE CHARACTER

One of the most remarkable of these men from a representative point of view is Gideon the son of Joash. The remarkable thing about him is not his achievements; it is his character, and it is that character which we propose to study. To learn how a man is representative of humanity we ought to forget his special environment. So shall we do with Gideon. We shall forget, as much as possible, his local surroundings. We shall forget "the Midianites" and "the Amalekites" and "the Children of the East." We shall forget the prescribed method by which he was to save Israel. We shall remember only that he was called to deliver his age from darkness and to lift his country from corruption. We shall try to lay our hand on that in him which is universal, permanent, liable to be repeated in all the coming years.

At first sight the character of Gideon is a very inconsistent one. It seems to be composed of two opposite sides—towering aspiration and drooping humility. On the one hand we see a man aflame with a great ideal and restless under its pressure. He has a prompting angel who is ever pointing him upward. He looks upon his sordid and benighted countrymen, and there floats before his eyes the possibility of becoming their redeemer. He feels that their present position is incongruous with their past history.

Are these the men that were brought up out of the land of Egypt? Are these the men that were kept alive in the desert by the direct power of God? Where are the signs of such a guidance; where is the evidence of such a protective care? If he, as a son of Israel, has been thus privileged, should he not live worthy of his privileges? Was it not his duty to aim at the high standard set before him, to lift up others to that standard? Had not his very nationality given him a mission, made it incumbent on him to fight the battles of the Lord? Was there not imposed on him a great, a responsible destiny—a destiny which he must not seek to evade? Was he not bound to become the savior of Israel?

GIDEON'S HUMILITY

So speaks the one side of his nature—the aspiring side. But there is another side. This same Gideon is the most humble of men—the most shrinking, the most cowering, the most timorous. Our very introduction to him finds him in a timid attitude—hiding in a cellar from marauding bands. He is deeply impressed with the thought of his own incompetency. He realizes the poverty of his family, the small repute of his kindred, the special insignificance which he himself exhibits in the eyes of his countrymen. His angel may applaud him, but his fellowmen decry him, and he feels that the voice of the men will drown the voice of the angel.

So far from trusting the voice of his angel, he asks material signs. In all ages—even the most modern—men in moments of self-doubt have resorted to these material signs. I knew a very distinguished student who had an extraordinary belief that his lucky number was thirteen. Instead of hoping for success on the ground of his own merits, he would become sanguine as to the receipt of university honors if, between certain points, he had happened to take just thirteen steps—neither less nor more. Gideon's signs are something of the same nature. "I will put my sacrifice on the fire; if the fire consume it quickly, I shall be a success." "I will leave a fleece exposed to the dew; if in the morning it is wet while all around is dry, I shall know that I am bound to win."

Now, on the part of the student and on the part of Gideon, this was very great humility. It was an absolute distrust of their own personality, an abandoning of all confidence in anything within them. The man whose faith in his good fortune rests on outward omens must be a very humble man. I return, then, to the question, how is this consistent with the other part of the character of Gideon? If he and the university student had been minds innately poor, we should not have marveled; but that a man capable of lofty aspirings should be as distrustful of himself as if he were a village rustic—this seems an unaccountable thing.

HUMILITY REQUIRES ENLIGHTENMENT

But is the village rustic distrustful of himself? That is the question, and in the answer to that question lies the solution of the whole mystery. I say that the village rustic, in proportion as his rusticity is deep, is increasingly removed from humility. Humility is incompatible with absolute ignorance. Little children are not humble. Why? Simply because humility requires some degree of enlightenment. Have we considered these words of the Master, "Blessed are the poor in spirit, for theirs is the kingdom of heaven" (Matt. 5:3)?

On what ground does He promise the kingdom to the consciously lowly? It is because the consciously lowly have already seen the kingdom, "Theirs is the kingdom." It is the vision of the kingdom that makes them lowly. It is their view of light on the hill that shows them the shades in the vale. It is by the sight of green fields that a man recognizes his gutter. It is by the hearing of sweet sounds that the ear learns surrounding discord. It is by the contact with pure souls that the heart finds the presence of its own sin.

There is, then, no contradiction but a beautiful harmony between the two sides of Gideon's character. So far from interfering with his humility, his aspirations are the cause of his humility; without these aspirations his humility would not exist. It is the brightness of his ideal that makes him shrink in dismay. He beats upon his breast and cries, "Unclean!" but he does so in the temple of God. He says, "Depart from me, for I am a sinful man, O Lord!"—but he says so in the presence of the Lord. All the misery about his personal state, all the tossings and tempests of his soul, come by his own admission from his vision of the angel. He recognizes the night after he has seen the day.

GIDEON'S MINISTRY TO HIS PEOPLE

When Gideon has set himself right, he proceeds to set right his people. Where does he begin? Is it by casting out their enemies? Is it by improving their environment? Is it by clearing from their path the outward sources of temptation? No, it is by changing their ideal of God. Gideon knew well that all bad things originate in bad thoughts. He begins, therefore, with the thoughts and with those thoughts the most central of all—the thoughts about God.

A man's ideal of religion is the root of his whole conduct. A bad ideal of religion is worse than no religion at all. Atheism pure and simple would in my opinion be merely paralyzing; it would be what Paul attributes to the climax of trespasses and sins—a state of deadness. But the belief in a bad God is not a state of deadness; it is not even a loss of energy. A bad ideal may lend to a man a lurid strength, may fill him with a life and power as vivid and as dangerous as the drunkard's delirium.

The peril of Israel at this period was not irreligion; it was too much religion of a bad kind. She had conceived a low ideal of God, a low ideal of what it is to be Divine. She had begun to worship Baal. To worship Baal was to worship sensuousness, if not sensuality. It was to reverence above all things the bodily nature of man—the lust of the flesh and the lust of the eye and the pride of life. It was to reverence the pursuit of animal pleasures and the exercise of animal strength. It was to reverence the oppression of the weak by the strong, the reign of violence, and the empire of physical force.

Hosea says, "The just will walk by their faith" (14:9). "Their ideal will make them just." But the other side is equally true—that the unjust will live by their faith. A man whose ideal of the Divine is Baal will be made unjust by his faith as surely as a Christian is justified by his. All badness, as well as all goodness, is the fruit of an idea. We are purified or defiled at the fountain—in the thought, the ideal. Gideon begins at the fountain. He sets himself to dispel their false ideal.

GIDEON SHOWS THE FEEBLENESS OF BAAL

How can he better dispel it than by associating it with feebleness! He will show that so far from protecting them, Baal cannot protect himself. Gideon will break Baal's image; he will cut down Baal's groves, he will prove the emptiness of Baal's shrine. But even in his moment of zeal, there is a reassertion of his native timidity. He is afraid to break the image in the light of day; he fears to cut down the groves while it is noon. He will wait for the hush of night. He will tarry till the world is asleep and the pulse of humanity beats low. Then he will sally forth in the silence and in the solitude, and, unseen by man, he will do the work for God.

And here there presents itself to my mind a great artistic contrast. The form of Gideon stands over against another figure—that of Elijah. There is just so much resemblance between them as to emphasize the difference. Both are animated by a horror of idolatry, and both have transmitted their name as the breakers of idols. Yet the course of their progress is very different—indeed, opposite. I would call Gideon an inverted Elijah.

Elijah is a man of fire to whom grace comes in the form of timidity; Gideon is a man of timidity to whom grace comes in the form of fire. Elijah begins in full flame and gradually mellows down; Gideon begins in trembling and gradually gathers heat. Elijah bursts upon our view in the court of Ahab—

in the glare of notoriety and the blaze of public opinion; but we find him afterwards collapsing in the cave of Horeb and experiencing the truth that the course of life's chariot does not run smooth. Gideon first comes before us under the shadow of night—lurking in secrecy and hiding in humility; but he ends where Elijah began—in the full view of all Israel and at the right hand of power.

GIDEON'S POWER IS THE POWER OF THE SPIRIT

The first step to Gideon's success is effected not by material force but by the power of the Spirit. When the worshipers of Baal come to his shrine in the morning, they find Baal's sanctuary in ruins. They have no doubt that the perpetrator of the sacrilege is Gideon.

Why, then, do they not put him to death? The answer given by the narrative is at once clear and striking; it is the very ruin of the shrine of Baal that makes them despise their idol. They cannot adore weakness, even in their God. The Roman could; he could allow Vulcan to have a lame foot and Cupid a blind eye. But then, the Roman worshiped the power of endurance, and power of endurance is compatible with calamity.

The worshiper of the physical cannot adore calamity. Whatever mars the symmetry of sight is by him condemned. The fall of Baal described in the picture is a fall from the heights of the heart. It is a mental process. Gideon has shown Baal's impotence. Gideon has battered down Baal's altars. Gideon has mutilated Baal's image. Gideon has cut Baal's groves in pieces.

Has Gideon suffered for the crime? Has lightning struck him? Has the blast withered him? Has the pestilence assailed him? No, he is alive and well; he has proved the victor, the uninjured combatant. If Baal had been able to punish Gideon, Baal would have punished him; if Baal cannot avenge his own wrongs, he is unfit to protect Israel.

GIDEON'S CONFIDENCE IN DIVINE POWER

The effect of this silence of Baal is the assembling of multitudes around the banner of Gideon. His ranks swell from day-to-day until his adherents number thirty-two thousand. He resolves to proceed from the expulsion of false ideals to the expulsion of their worshipers. It is at this stage that he passes from the life of the devotee into the life of the warrior, and he carries into the life of the warrior the humility which has marked his life of devotion.

Before going forth to make war on the corrupters of the land, Gideon takes an extraordinary step—a step which can only be understood in the light of his native lowliness of mind. He reduces his thirty-two thousand men to three hundred. The act seems at first sight to display extreme confidence, a spirit of arrogant self-assurance. But if you look deeper, you will see that it springs from the utter abandonment of self, from the determination to dispel the glory of his own name.

If he goes out with thirty-two thousand men, the victory will be attributed to the arm of Israel. He is jealous for God, jealous for the manifestation of the divine power. He will not suffer human agencies to bear the credit of that help which comes from God alone. He will not have men say, "Israel triumphed by her splendid resources, by her vast numbers, by her well-appointed army." He will prevent them from saying so. He will reduce his material strength. He will bury his deadliest weapons. He will dismiss the bulk of his fighting men. He will go forth to battle accompanied by only a handful. So will he prove conclusively that the secret of his strength has been God alone.

This is very much what Paul means by saying, "We have our treasure in earthen vessels." The idea is that in any hour of success our richest religious comfort comes from our sense of inability to have produced that success. It is quite possible, indeed, that in the hour of his triumph a man may say, "I always knew I was clever!"—it is quite possible and it is quite legitimate. But this is not a religious comfort.

The religious comfort of any success is the sense that I have had nothing to do with it, that my resources were inadequate to achieve it. The more its accomplishment has been removed from human power, the more we see God in it—the more we recognize in it the working of a divine will. And what is true of outward success is not less true in a region which is still nearer to Christian experience—the region of inward peace. Let me explain what I mean.

INWARD PEACE

Paul says that the peace of God is distinguished from all other kinds of peace in that it "passeth understanding" (Phil. 4:7). He means to say that it cannot be explained on any natural principles. It has the capacity of entering the heart when all the avenues are closed—when the doors are shut, when the windows are shut, when the apertures are hermetically sealed. There are very few of us who have not had this experience. There have been times when to the eye of all the world we have seemed to be absolutely miserable—times when, by any human calculation, we ought to be absolutely miserable. Clouds and darkness are round about us; thorns and briers surround our way.

And yet, the strange thing is that our aspect of absolute misery is deceptive. We are not miserable—in spite of the clouds and darkness, in spite of the thorns and briers. We feel an unaccountable strength, an inexplicable support. It has come when heart and flesh have failed in themselves to find any remedy. It has come with a sense of surprise—like the advent of an unexpected guest.

It is the feeling which I attribute to the Psalmist when he utters the words, "Thou hast put gladness in my heart more than in the time when corn and wine increased" (Ps. 4:7). He is crying out with wonder. He is expressing astonishment. Notwithstanding his outward causes for depression, he feels happier than he was when he was pointed to as a favorite of fortune. His experience seems to contradict his environment. He ought to feel heavy hearted; his heart is light. Surely this is a strength coming from above!

Now, every religious man wants to have this experience. It is the greatest argument for the supernatural which human life reveals—an argument founded on no theory, on no dogma, on no flight of fancy but on sober and positive fact. It is no wonder that Gideon wished to have this experience. That he did wish to have it is beyond all question. It was this which made him reduce his thirty-two thousand to three hundred. He said to himself, "I want to have an evidence of God in my life. I want to have a peace that passeth understanding—a peace that shall be established by no big battalions, by no preponderance of material strength, by no superiority in the physical weapons of conquest but in spite of the absence of these. I want the kingdom of righteousness to triumph through means unknown to me, uncalculated by me. I must be able to feel in my hour of victory that I have been fighting God's battle and that God has won it. How shall I learn this if my natural arm is strong and my natural force unabated! Only under the shadow of my own night shall I have evidence of the heavenly star; only by my own nothingness shall I recognize the will of God!"

HUMILITY A SOURCE OF CONFIDENCE

Here is a great paradox—humility made a source of confidence! But it is a paradox which has its ground in truth. Timid men are humble, but humble men need not be timid. There is a humility which makes us bold—Christian humility does. What does Paul mean by saying that where he is weak there he is strong? He means, "My greatest confidence comes from the fact that I have succeeded in doing things which to me were impossible—above my talent, beyond my capacity; by this I know that God is working for me and in me."

Take any period of your life in which you have felt a supreme confidence in a guiding divine hand. What has been the ground of that confidence? Simply the fact that your success in the past has been no work of yours. You feel that you have been a poor creature without adequate knowledge or adequate foresight, yet you are conscious that you have climbed heights beyond your natural power and plucked fruits beyond your natural reach. You say, "I have been guided all through yesterday by a power and in a way which I cannot comprehend; may I not trust, under the same impending cloud, that the hand which led me yesterday will guide me through tomorrow?"

A PRAYER

Lord, give me the peace of Gideon! Give me the peace of mind that can subsist amid stress of body; give me the calm of soul that can live amid storms of sea! Often is Your peace bestowed when the world's peace is denied. Often my heart, like Gideon's, sees the thirty-two thousand melt into the three hundred.

Make my heart like the strength of Gideon! Send me the calm that cannot be accounted for! Send me the peace that cannot be explained! Send me the joy which the world cannot justify! Send me the gladness independent of glitter, the radiance independent of riches, the brightness independent of earthly benefits!

Reveal Your rest in my wrestling, Your crown in my cross, Your kingdom in my cloud! Let there ever be a dove in my deluge! Let Your Spirit brood on the face of my waters and say to all the chaos, "Let there be light!" Let Your light precede the green grass, precede the herb and plant and tree! Let it come before the flowers come, before the fruits come! Let it shine while my world is yet a wilderness, while as yet no vines have enriched my field! So shall I learn that Your peace is a peace that passeth understanding.

For Further Study and Reflection

1. What was Gideon called by God to do?
2. What is the difference between humilty and ignorance?
3. Why is a bad religion—a low ideal of God—worse than no religion at all?
4. Explain Paul's statement, "We have our treasures in earthen vessels."
5. How does our richest religious comfort come from our inability to produce our own success?